MW00425420

Psalms in the Key of Healing

Jewish Life, Death, and Transition Series

Other Titles from the Series

Psalms in the Key of Healing

A Text Study for Clergy, Chaplains and People Living with Illness

Edited by
Rabbi H. Rafael Goldstein
with Rabbi J.B. Sacks

Foreword by
Rabbi Joseph Telushkin *&* Chaplain Dvorah Telushkin

Albion
Andalus

Boulder, Colorado
2021

"The old shall be renewed,
and the new shall be made holy."
— Rabbi Avraham Yitzhak Kook

Copyright © 2021 H. Rafael Goldstein
First edition. All rights reserved.

No part of this book may be reproduced or transmitted in
any form or by any means, electronic or mechanical, including
photocopy, recording, or any information storage or retrieval
system, except for brief passages in connection with a critical
review, without permission in writing from the publisher:

Albion-Andalus, Inc.
P. O. Box 19852
Boulder, CO 80308
www.albionandalus.com

Design and composition by **Albion-Andalus Books**
Cover design by **D.A.M. Cool Graphics**
Cover image is a detail from a Coptic/Sahidic psalter codex
held at the University of Pennsylvania Museum in Philadelphia.

ISBN-13: 978-1-953220-04-2

Manufactured in the United States of America

To my siblings:
Clifford and Paula Goldstein,
who have been here for me every step.

Anne and Howard Dobelle,
who have taken such good care of me in my illness.

Janet Cooper,
who baked and provided practical help
when I needed it.

Dr. David and Minka Goldstein,
who have brought healing to others.

To Professor Gwyn Davies,
the best friend I could ever have!

Contents

Acknowledgements

Rabbi Dr. Richard Address served as a mentor for the original doctoral project and has encouraged me ever since. Paula Goldstein read the manuscript before anyone else and supported my writing throughout. She really improved the text. Rabbi Gloria S. Rubin spent countless hours editing and advising and her help made all the difference!

— H.R.G.

Rabbi Goldstein died prior to the publication of his work. We are therefore indebted to his friend and fellow contributor, Rabbi J.B. Sacks, for his dedication in shepherding the project to completion, as well as his friend, Ben Zion Kogen, who checked the Hebrew and Hebrew transliterations.

— The Publisher

Foreword

Rabbi Joseph Telushkin &
Chaplain Dvorah Telushkin

Next to the Torah, the book of Psalms—whose 150 psalms are the most famous religious poems ever written—has probably inspired more books, commentaries, and volumes of sermons than any of the other biblical books. In addition, selections from the book of Psalms form the backbone of the Siddur, the Hebrew prayer book.

And now a new book about the psalms has come out, and I can say with confidence that Rabbi Dr. H Rafael Goldstein's *Psalms in the Key of Healing: A Text Study for Clergy, Chaplains, and People Living with Illness* (with contributions by Rabbi Dr. Richard Address, Rabbi Dayle Friedman, Cantor Rabbi Dr. Rhoda Harrison, Rabbi Dr. J.B. Sacks, and Rabbi Dr. Shira Stern), is, in my view, one of the most important works on psalms written in many decades. I believe this is true for two reasons in particular.

First, Psalms is a book that lends itself to study by Jews as well as Christians. I would guess that the percentage of Christians who are familiar with the 23rd Psalm, "The Lord is my Shepherd" is as high as it is among Jews. Rabbi Goldstein cites the story of Daniel, an evangelical Christian who wanted to hear the words that matched his own conclusions about life: "We are all walking together in the 'valley of the shadow of death'" These words are, of course, also drawn from the 23rd Psalm.

Second, in addition to its impact on Protestant and Catholic Christians, the Psalms also resonate with Muslims and Buddhists. I can say with pride (a pride reinforced by reading this book) that Psalms is one of Judaism's great gifts to the world. As Rabbi Goldstein recounts inside: "I presented Psalm 27 to an interfaith clergy group, faith leaders from Harlem, one an imam." He heard echoes from the Psalms in the Qur'an. A Buddhist monk related the text to his tradition. The themes are universal. All of us experience grief, shame, forgiveness, hope and joy.

How does the aforementioned Psalm 27 begin? "God is my light and help, whom should I fear?" While people sometimes do not like to speak about fear/awe of God, feeling that it makes religion sound primitive, the Hebrew Bible acknowledges that fear/awe of God can also be a liberating emotion. When Pharaoh decreed that all newborn Israelite infants were to be cast into the Nile, the people who disobeyed Pharaoh's edict were two midwives who, the Bible explains, "feared/were in awe of God." The rest of the Egyptians went along with the edict because they feared Pharaoh—it was the fear/awe of God that liberated the midwives from the fear of Pharaoh. The whole 27th Psalm is a testament to the fear/awe of God's ability to liberate us from fear of other human beings and, as this extraordinary book teaches, can sometimes even help liberate us from the fear/awe of illness and death.

A stunning recollection by Rabbi Goldstein helped bring me to an understanding of an issue I have long struggled with: Is it really possible, is it really reasonable, to ask people to forgive those who have done an act that should, at least in my view, be regarded as unforgivable? Listen to Rabbi Goldstein's take on this issue:

> When I presented "The Dynamics of Forgiveness" to the National Association of Jewish Chaplains (of which I became the

Executive Director 10 years later), it did not go well. One of the people in the presentation said that her ex-husband molested their son; she could never forgive him for that, and I should not ask her to. Another person immediately went to Hitler. Thus, I learned to talk about the "unforgivable."

Here comes Goldstein's stunning insight: "But the language of forgiveness is part of the problem. We often think forgiveness is reconciliation. We don't have a good word for 'letting go of the anger,' for the forgiveness that has little to do with the person who did us harm. The anger eats us up, not the person we are angry at."

Forgiveness sometimes—one hopes—means reconciliation; sometimes there is no room for reconciliation, but there can be room for letting go. Goldstein teaches that well.

Because of this book, the eternal words of the Psalms can become household words. Their lyrics and poetry can resonate in the hearts and in the mouths of clergy and laity and all people in need of healing.

As the Hafetz Hayyim comments on the final verse in the 23rd Psalm: "May goodness and kindness pursue me all the days of my life…" The Hafetz Hayyim also notes: "We are all destined to be pursued in our lives, some of us by illness, some of us by criminals, and some of us by debt collectors." "Blessed are those pursued by acts of goodness, charity and kindness."

Introduction

Daniel

I went to Daniel's room because he was on the cardiac unit, which I was covering. That meant I was visiting people who were awake and had not specifically said they did not want a Spiritual Care visit. I knew Daniel might be receptive, since there were notes in his chart that indicated he was "Catholic," and that he had no religion. I figured I might as well assess whether he needed a priest to visit.

Daniel welcomed me into his room. I asked him what was going on. He told me that he'd had a heart transplant twenty years ago, and now the heart was being rejected by his body. He was waiting for a new transplant, but in the meantime, an LVAD (left ventricular assist device) had been implanted into his chest, to help the heart that was no longer working properly. He sounded pretty optimistic about the chances of a heart being found to replace the one that replaced his original heart.

I asked Daniel about his religion. He said he had none but was raised Catholic. He told me his sister was a "right-wing evangelical Christian" and wanted him to join her in this religious perspective. He indicated that was not for him. While he did not want to return to the Catholic Church, he felt very connected to God, Jesus, and the spiritual beliefs he had grown up with. I asked what I could do to help him spiritually. He asked me to read Psalm 23.

1

Psalms in the Key of Healing

I was shocked by the request. It was so specific, and the 23rd Psalm is so associated with death, I was concerned he was indicating something to me about his fears. I read the psalm to him, then I asked him what it meant to him. Daniel told me it was about hope for him, that he would live with God in eternity. That thought brought him comfort, no matter what happens with the replacement heart.

He asked me what the psalm meant to me. I affirmed what he said and added there are a lot of things happening in this psalm. I asked him about the Valley of the Shadow of Death. Where/what was it for him? He said he never thought about it. We discussed possibilities. Ultimately, he decided that all of life is in that valley: we are all walking together in the shadow of death. It was a meaningful discussion for both of us.

As the weeks went by, I continued to visit Daniel. Every week, he would ask me to read a psalm, and would then say, "Okay rabbi, what's it about?" I always tried to get him to answer his own question, and we would discuss the psalm and his interpretation. He was not getting any better, and the prospect of a new heart was not very promising. We discussed the possibility of him getting a new heart, and the possibility that he would not. He said he knew it was risky, and he remained optimistic, but he was also very much aware that his life was at risk. He said he was ready for whatever happens. When I asked what that meant, he told me he had no idea.

Daniel's condition deteriorated, and he became too weak and too sick to survive a transplant. Even when he was barely conscious, he would ask me to read him a psalm. He stopped telling me what it meant for him, but I continued to struggle with the interpretation for him, to make the psalm relevant to his situation. He knew he was going to die, relatively soon, and that he would finally stop suffering. When he could no longer speak, and I was unsure of how conscious he was, I continued to read psalms to him, and to tell him what I thought each psalm was about. Though it was no longer a discussion, I assumed the interactions were comforting.

Daniel's sister told me she wanted him to convert to her born-again Christianity, and did everything she could to keep him alive, even when it was clear that the process was prolonging his suffering, not his living. Daniel had designated her as his health-care proxy, and even though he did not want to prolong his suffering, she was making decisions for him based on her belief system. She believed everything possible should be done to keep him alive, well beyond the time when there was any chance for quality of life or recovery. Daniel died a few months after I met him.

Reading and discussing Psalms brought him comfort and strength. Maybe it also helped him to know that I would keep coming back, and that we would always have something to discuss.

Rebecca

I went to Rebecca's room because a nurse suggested she could use some spiritual care—she was in pain and refusing to take pain medications. Rebecca welcomed me and told me that she was a Pentecostal Bishop; her church was on the Upper East Side of New York City. I asked how she was doing with her illness. She sighed and said she saw her suffering as only a tiny fraction of how Jesus suffered. She welcomed the pain because it brought her closer to understanding Jesus, to feeling his presence, to being one with him.

I noticed the Bible on her bed—it was open to Psalm 27. I asked her if she was praying with Psalm 27. She told me that the last line brought her comfort. "Wait on the Lord: be of good courage, and he shall strengthen thine heart: wait, I say, on the Lord." I told Rebecca that the Hebrew word for "hope" was translated here as "wait". We discussed the difference between the two words, and that waiting seemed so passive.

3

Then Rebecca told me that she didn't know there was a Hebrew version of the book of Psalms. She had only read it in her Bible (King James Version, though she did not seem to be aware of the word "version"), and that the words in her Bible were the words of God. She never thought about these words being a translation/interpretation of the words of God. As she understood it, the Bible was always in the language she read and was literally accurate. Rebecca didn't think there was any room for interpretation. The literal meaning is clear to her. She would wait for the Lord, patiently.

I would never want to threaten anyone else's theology, so I apologized for not being aware of her perspective. I asked her to read the Psalm to me, which she did, with tears in her eyes. I asked her what it meant to her. She said it meant a lot to share the words of God with someone from a different religion, and that, in her pain the Psalm brought her hope and serenity. She was waiting for God to do what God was going to do. I asked Rebecca about her fears. She said she was not afraid, because God was with her; whatever happens is God's will.

I asked her how she would bless someone from her congregation in her situation. She recited a blessing for healing, in the name of Jesus. I added "May this be Your will, Holy One."

Rebecca dedicated her life to serving God, and saw no fracture in that relationship because of her illness. She saw the illness as bringing her wisdom and strength through her pain. Reading Psalms brought her calm and reinforcement for her relationship with God, enhancing her trust in the relationship.

David

David was in recovery for drug abuse in the mental health wing of the hospital. The hospital did not usually get involved in recovery from drug abuse, so it was odd for him to be on this floor, which was locked. David was about 35-years old, Jewish, and looked well-groomed when I met him. We chatted in the courtyard outside of the ward. He told me that he could not forgive himself for all the terrible things he had done. I asked him, "Like what?" And he went through an entire list, which included lies, cheating, and a lot of thievery. He told me he had once stolen $15 from his mother's wallet as a teenager. That was the worst part for him, that he had fractured his relationship with his mother and had started his "life of crime" by robbing his own mother. "How can I ever forgive myself for that?" he asked me.

David was sad and unwilling to forgive himself. I reminded him that we, as Jews, are forgiven for all the terrible things we have done every year on Yom Kippur. "God doesn't hold grudges," I said. God wants us to move on and do better next time. No matter how terrible our behavior, God is waiting for us to repent, and is ready to forgive us; we are supposed to follow in God's proverbial footsteps! If God can forgive, we can forgive. So, why are you holding on to the unforgivable? Did you think your mother is holding a grudge about $15 twenty years later?"

But David had spent a lot of time investing in self-hatred, and it was clear that he was going to hold on to that bitterness and self-loathing. He remained in the hospital for more than a month, giving me an opportunity to visit him a few times. On my third visit, I asked if he had ever read the Psalms. He said he had not done anything Jewish since his bar mitzvah, but he was open to it. We looked at Psalm 103 and focused on the issues of God's forgiveness in the psalm. I asked him how he would feel if he knew God had forgiven him. He said he would be grateful, and maybe that could start something new in him. I asked if he felt that the people he had wronged would ultimately forgive him. I pointed out that as he works through the "12 Steps," he will have to make a list of all the things he had done, and to seek forgiveness from the people involved. He said he knew he would have to do that, which is one of the reasons he didn't feel ready to go to any Narcotics Anonymous (NA) groups. We talked more about forgiveness and my hope that he would find his way to self-forgiveness as well. I pointed out, in case he had missed it, that God had forgiven him long ago. All he needed to do was to believe it!

I learned from David that the issue of forgiveness begins first with forgiving ourselves. While we can learn that God is not holding grudges, letting go of our own grudges can be much more difficult. A God who is "compassionate and gracious, slow to anger, abounding in steadfast love" is nice, but may not be enough until (or unless) we are willing to have the same compassion for ourselves.

Reading Psalm 103 and affirming that God had forgiven him wasn't enough for David, but it did serve as a jumping off point, a place where we could get into his own role in holding on to his self-loathing. But in this case, we will never know if there were any results. As a chaplain, I thought it was a worthwhile experiment, to show David that he was not the first person (nor will he be the last), to struggle with forgiveness, to normalize the struggle through reflection on the words of the psalm.

Bonnie

When I was paged to visit Bonnie in her hospital room, the nurse asked to speak with me first. I met with the nurse, who told me that Bonnie had a rare neurological disorder which made her skin incredibly sensitive, and she could not have anything touching her skin, thus she was naked in her bed, uncovered. I thought about what to do: there was no way I could meet with a patient who was so exposed. I decided this was a teaching opportunity. I asked one of my students to accompany me, so I would not be alone in the room with the patient. Then I asked the nurse to let Bonnie know we were coming into her room and would be sitting on the other side of the privacy curtain, to ensure her dignity and privacy. I introduced myself and my student to Bonnie and asked what was going on.

Bonnie said she was grateful we found a way to talk; a curtain, she said, was better than a phone call. Bonnie acknowledged the student's presence, and I told her that the student was there to observe the conversation, and to learn from it. Bonnie told me about life with this neurological condition. For her, it was absolutely terrible. The pain was unbearable at times, and there were so many people who could not find ways to communicate with her because she had to be naked all the time. She noted that it made other people really uncomfortable, including her siblings (she was not in a relationship with anyone outside of her family).

Bonnie told me how isolated she felt. She used to go to church, and loved the music, the companionship, and the community. But she was not feeling a lot of support from her church now. She did not feel she could ask for it, either, as she was embarrassed to explain what was happening with her. And she certainly could not tell her pastor, she said. She sounded sad and alone, and we talked about her sadness and isolation for a while.

Eventually, I asked her if there was a hymn, a psalm, or a reading she particularly liked from church. Without hesitation she said "Psalm 121" and began reciting it— "The LORD shall preserve thy going out and thy coming in from this time forth, and even for evermore."

I asked what that meant to her now. "Despite everything," she said, "I feel God is there for me, and will protect me . . . Just like you figuring out a way for us to talk, without either of us feeling uncomfortable." She said that was God protecting her.

I asked if there were other ways in which she felt God's presence in this illness. She expressed gratitude for the nurses and doctors who were helping her, as God's representatives. I noted that this illness was certainly not what she wanted or needed, but it sounded like it was an opportunity for learning, growing, and feeling God's Presence.

Before leaving, I asked her if she would like a blessing, and asked what she would want to pray for. I blessed her and watched her heave a sigh of relief. I asked her how the blessing felt to her, and she began to cry. She had really missed going to church, and missed feeling blessed by that experience. I expressed my hope that she would be able to get back to church again soon. I also suggested calling her pastor and discussing her illness with him. Perhaps he could also find a way of bringing her blessings without either of them feeling uncomfortable. She said she would call him.

Bonnie was discharged from the hospital the next day, so I never got to follow up with her. I did ask the student who joined us for her reflections on the experience. She noted that she thought speaking through the curtain was a good idea and asked whether it would have been appropriate for her, as a woman, to go on the other side of the curtain. I told her that gender did not matter in this case: there would never be a reason for a chaplain to be in a room with a naked and exposed patient—the dignity of the patient comes first. The student also asked if it would have been appropriate to reach behind the curtain to hold the patient's hand at any time. I told her that since we did not know exactly where the bed was, and where the patient was, it would probably not work. But I also noted that the neurological disorder made anything touching her skin painful. We could not know whether that included her hands. I suggested that if Bonnie wanted us to hold hands, she would have said so, and could have told us how to make it happen.

Barbara

I met with Barbara in a residential hospice facility. She was clearly living her last days of life. While she was conscious and able to speak, it was hard for her. She told me she had been a musician and had written and recorded the album which was playing in the background. It was nice, calming music, with lyrics in Hebrew. As a music therapist, she did a lot of work with people who were dying. She was proud of helping people who would die soon to feel a little bit better in their process. Barbara was in her early 50's and told me she had end-stage breast cancer. We talked about some of her work, and the intersections between her work and mine. It was a meaningful discussion for me, and I hope it was for her.

During a lull in the conversation, listening to the music, I could not help but notice the words of the song were Psalm 150, in which almost every verse begins with "Praise God." This psalm is part of the liturgy for most Jewish services. Barbara's version of the music was beautiful. I told her so, and asked how she chose this psalm to be a part of her album for people who were dying.

Barbara responded that she heard so many people expressing so much gratitude during their last days: gratitude for the gentle care they were receiving; gratitude for the family around; gratitude for the life they led. I asked her if she was grateful. She made a face (sort of *duh!*) and said of course she was grateful. I asked "For what?" She responded with tears "That my parents are not alive to see me die." I asked about them and her relationship with each parent.

I asked, "What else?" She listed many things about her life and accomplishments. She told me how she got into working with people who were dying, and about her musical history. She said she was really proud to have accomplished so much in her life. Then said she was grateful for having the opportunity to think about what she was grateful for at this time in her life. It was nice for her to list the good things she had experienced, even as her future was so limited. Barbara gave me a copy of her CD. She had a few of them in the drawer next to her bed. She thanked me for coming, and I sang her a blessing. She died the next morning.

Chaplains and Psalms

The interactions with Daniel, Rebecca, David, Bonnie, and Barbara, led me to wonder how our Clinical Pastoral Education (CPE) students were doing with patients for whom psalms were meaningful.

This book began as my doctoral project at Hebrew Union College/JIR. But it became clear to me, as I taught psalms to chaplaincy students, interfaith clergy, and chaplains at national conferences that I needed to translate the dialogue on the psalms into a book that could be useful for others. I noted that while many people have read the psalms, and many are familiar with the text of various psalms, in-depth study of their words, and their implications for life and death issues was missing from the education. In fact, while this started as a project to educate chaplains, it became quite clear early on that there was a need to share these psalms with others, with people who are not chaplains or clergy.

This book begins with chaplains and chaplaincy education. As many non-chaplains have no idea what chaplaincy education and training consists of, I will describe it, and some of the interface between chaplains and the psalms. If you are not that interested in chaplains, no worries! It is only where I start, not where I end.

Come with me on the journey! I start with chaplains, but this book is for everyone, of all backgrounds, religions, professions, orientations. Don't get too hung up on the chaplain/patient interactions; see them as the starting point for this project. You can easily substitute the words "chaplain" and "patient" with other helping and caring relationships.

Chaplains and Patients

The theological background of CPE (Clinical Pastoral Education) students varies greatly, given that students can come from a wide range of experience, religious backgrounds, and training. While some students may be entering a second or third career, others may be entering the field of chaplaincy at the beginning of their professional experience. First and foremost, training varies based on religion, and depends on the seminary or school of theology that a student might have attended. Some students are ordained or in some other way endorsed by a religious institution; some come from faith backgrounds with no such formal structures. For example, Catholic women cannot be ordained within their faith, and their theological education would likely have been through other denominations or interfaith programs. Imams are not ordained, adding another level of complexity to their educational background, and many other religions do not have educational opportunities for training their leaders in a formal manner. While some traditions encourage hermeneutics, others show preference for unquestioning loyalty to the word as it appears on a page or as interpreted by religious leaders.

Because of the tremendous range of backgrounds from which students come, chaplaincy training focuses on honing and using their empathetic listening skills to encourage patients to find meaning, strength, and wisdom, even when their lives are challenged and when they might be afraid. While there is a secondary focus of helping patients explore their own spirituality and theology as related to illness, CPE curricula often do not use any traditional texts. Prayer is usually spontaneous, built by a chaplain together with the patient, petitioning the Holy One for help or strength, expressing gratitude or a patient's emotional needs.

The hardest thing for Jewish chaplains to learn seems to be spontaneous prayer. Jews are so used to everything coming out of printed pages. The idea of spontaneous prayer can be both liberating and daunting. When someone who has only used prayer books for prayer is asked to create his/her own prayer, it is totally disorienting. Yet it also could be very meaningful, once a person gets the hang of it. The vast majority of Jewish chaplains first turn to printed blessings—whatever they can find in a book, any book. It takes much more work to learn to trust that even if it is not printed, prayer can be meaningful, maybe even more so than a printed prayer.

My rabbinical school classmate, Rabbi Bonita Taylor, BCC/ ACPE taught, "Ask people what they would like to pray for." Chaplains can be very surprised by the answers, which may or may not arise from the conversation prior to the blessing. But when a chaplain uses the thoughts and words of the person for whom they are praying, the prayer becomes incredibly powerful and affirming.

The CPE curriculum recognizes that patients may read Psalms or other traditional texts from their religious backgrounds, but there is no formal training in understanding what the patients might experience reading Psalms or attempt to reconcile traditional texts with the CPE curriculum. Yet patients turn to chaplains as spiritual guides, and often expect chaplains to use and comment on materials from their own spiritual backgrounds or experience. Very often patients bring their own Bibles from home, or request them from the Department of Spiritual Care, and the books are open to Psalms or other passages that might bring some comfort to the patient. Chaplains tend to note that the text is there and open, but rarely discuss the content or meaning of the text for the patient.

To become a Board-Certified Chaplain, a student must log 1600 clinical and supervisory/class hours, function as a chaplain for at least 2000 additional hours, and prepare materials and essays for a Board Interview. Yet, during all of this training, discussion of traditional texts, and of the themes of grief/loss, hope, shame, forgiveness and gratitude may not be discussed in terms of patient's experience or using a traditional text to help a patient process their feelings.

I could not envision doing all those hours without pay and gave up on the idea of becoming a chaplain until I got a job at the San Diego Jewish Federation as the Jewish Community Chaplain. They hired me before I had any official qualifications.

I was an intern, and then a resident at Sharp Memorial Hospital, and thank Rev. James Corrigan, ACPE, and Rev. John Breding, ACPE, for being incredible mentors and teachers, and all of my colleagues in the program.

While there are very few textbooks for the CPE curriculum, and every CPE program functions differently, the Association for Clinical Pastoral Education (ACPE) accredits CPE programs. There are rigorous standards and policies that must be met, and every CPE program develops its minimum curriculum to meet these standards, which include: interfaith awareness and respect for individual religious perspectives, pastoral formation, pastoral competence, and pastoral reflection. The ACPE does not mandate how any of this is accomplished. Traditional text study is not a component of the ACPE requirements and is generally not a component of the CPE curriculum, unless a student presents a text as a student-led didactic or worship program.

In general, the theological component of the CPE curriculum is based on personal experience, or a lack of experience, of God's Presence in one's life. It revolves around finding the holiness in personal stories, and the struggle to find meaning in life, suffering, human experience, as drawn from personal interactions. While there may be references to books on Theology, and discussion of religious approaches to understanding theology, there is no textual study or opportunity for chaplains in this training to react to, consider, or work through the issues of any original source material, including materials which the patients may be turning to for comfort.

Chaplains value meeting a patient with "no agenda": to allow the patient to express him/herself fully, without the chaplain's imposition of preconceived notions or plans to "fix" anything. To achieve this, many chaplains believe they should enter a patient's room empty-handed, so the patient sees the chaplain is completely open to focus on the conversation without any ideas of what might be useful or worthwhile for them. The purpose of the Psalms project was not to change that approach in any way. However, if the chaplain were more informed about these traditional textual materials, and if the patient's issues and concerns were related, and if the patient was open to it, speaking a language that invites the use of Psalms or other traditional texts (e.g., why is God doing this to me?), chaplains could be informed and able to approach and utilize these and other texts.

On the other hand, patients who bring their Bibles with them from home are seeking, both as physical connection to their faith in a time of struggle (literally something to hold on to and see a connection with their Higher Power) and as a source of meaning. Many will turn to Psalms for comfort, strength, connection, and hope when hospitalized. Providing a frame of reference for dialogue on Psalms could be very helpful for chaplaincy students, especially when dealing with patients who are spiritually connected to a faith group or religion.

The chaplain may not answer the patients' theological questions for them, but is expected to explore the emotions around the existential and theological questions that patients raise. It is during this process of discussion and exploration that a chaplain may inform the discussion using concepts from the psalms.

Moving on From Chaplains

I learned in teaching these texts to chaplains, students, congregants, rabbis, priests, pastors, ministers, imams, and other religious leaders, that there was always a meaningful discussion, no matter who was engaged in the conversation. Looking at these ancient texts enables us to think about what we find meaningful—they help us define what we have in common, what unifies people in the struggle to understand that which is holy, and the mystery of illness as we looked at our personal theology, while expanding the horizons of understanding of both the texts and of ourselves. At times, the words of the texts became a jumping-off point for discussions that led to many other places and texts. There is a universal energy to struggling with these texts, and to finding the mysteries behind the letters of the texts.

"Psalm 27, Shame and Self-Acceptance" was presented in January, 2013, at the National Association of Jewish Chaplains conference in Scottsdale, Arizona. The response of the 43 Jewish chaplains who attended the workshop was enthusiastic and positive. They felt that the topic, material, and concept of teaching Psalms to chaplains (to clarify spiritual issues with patients) had significant merit. Interpreting the psalm in terms of a specific theme was seen as a very good idea, and there were no disagreements with the details of the interpretation or approach, which is quite an accomplishment with an audience of 43 chaplains, most of whom are rabbis!

Psalms 23 (Grief), 27 (Shame) and 103 (Forgiveness) were presented at national conferences of the Association for Professional Chaplains, and the National Association of Catholic Chaplains with similar positive responses.

When I presented "The Dynamics of Forgiveness" to the National Association of Jewish Chaplains (of which I became the Executive Director 10 years later), it did not go well. One of the people in the presentation said that her ex-husband molested their son; she could never forgive him for that, and I should not ask her to. Another person immediately went to Hitler. Thus, I learned to talk about the "unforgivable."

But the language of forgiveness is part of the problem. We often think forgiveness is reconciliation. We don't have a good word for "letting go of the anger," for the forgiveness that has little to do with the person who did us harm. The anger eats us up, not the person we are angry at.

The person in my presentation could and should never reconcile with her ex. That was not the issue. She needed to say that she could not change the history but could change the future by letting go of the anger, letting go of the hurt and moving on. Her ex was irrelevant. The only forgiveness that matters is the forgiveness we bless ourselves with by letting go of the hurt and anger. I will always be grateful to the person who shared her unforgivable story, so that I would be better able to talk about real forgiveness.

With the responses from each interfaith chaplains' conference, it became clear that writing the project up in the form of a book would be worthwhile. The big challenge was that the project was intended as a dialogue to engage people in discussion, and most people don't argue with their books. The project included lists of questions to address regarding each psalm. The important part was not my answers to these questions: it was the conversation about the questions. And there were no "Right Answers" for most questions raised.

The goal of this book then is to find ways to engage the reader without preaching, to get the reader to look at the issues raised and discuss them with someone. Ideally, this book should be read in small groups, or with study partners so there is opportunity to discuss, argue, and engage dynamically with the texts. Feel free to disagree with my opinions, my ideas and traditional interpretations—everything you might have ever thought about the texts. Approach the texts with your curiosity. I hope that each time you look at it, you will find yourself differing with your previous views!

Scuba Diving into the Psalms

We chose to take a very different approach to understanding these texts. The Jewish traditional approach would be to look at every commentary possible, from the first Midrashic writings to Talmudic references, from commentaries from the Middle Ages to all commentaries thereafter on each psalm. There is great wisdom in that approach, but the downside is the implication that people in different times had perspectives on these psalms which are more meaningful than our own thoughts and reactions. But just as they looked at the text and tried to make sense of it for themselves, we need to do that as well. Whatever a great sage wrote about the meaning of the words for him, in his time, does not define for us what we make of these same words, in our time. Maybe this book will inspire someone else to do all the research to see where our understandings converge and diverge with the hundreds of commentators who came before us. That is not the point of this book. This book is intended as a struggle of our own to understand the meaning of these words, for us, now, no matter how they were once interpreted.

I will present in this book the five psalms of the original project and have invited incredible authors to share their perspectives on their favorite or most compelling psalm. I have asked them to carefully translate the Hebrew into modern, meaningful English, and to help us all find the gems hidden in each word and phrase. Rabbi Dr. Richard Address, Rabbi Dayle Friedman, BCC, Cantor Dr. Rhoda Harrison, Rabbi Dr. J.B. Sacks and Rabbi Dr. Shira Stern, BCC have contributed their own perspectives through chapters in this book.

Ground Rules: Translations and Interpretations

In order to study these psalms as tools for eliciting emotions and experiences, the psalms must be translated from the original Hebrew for English-speaking participants (Although I did present Psalm 23 to two Hebrew speaking study groups in Israel. Much to my surprise, I was able to do it in Hebrew, and even make some sense!). The King James translation of the Bible seems to be the translation with which most people are familiar. The use of Old English lends the psalms a sense of being ancient, and there's a comfort and feeling of tradition for people who use this translation.

Unfortunately, the King James translation is woefully inaccurate in places. For instance, in Ps. 23, the King James Version translates the last line as: "Only goodness and mercy will follow me all the days of my life..." But the verb in Hebrew *(yirdifuni)* literally translated is "run after" or "chase." There is a huge difference between something following and something chasing. They may both be behind, but there's a very different intent to the verbs.

While many people have never experienced the Psalms in any other translation, it seemed important to use a text that was more accurate to the literal meaning of the words. The Jewish Publication Society's 1985 translation of the Tanakh (Jewish Holy Scripture) was the basis for many of the versions. However, there was interpretive wording even in this translation which obfuscated the meaning of some words. For instance, the Hebrew word *"ra"* literally means "bad" in Ps 23:4. The translation of *"ra"* according to JPS is "harm" and according to the King James, "evil". Evil adds a sinful connotation that may not be in the meaning of the text. "Harm" is too general a word and doesn't capture the concept either. "Malevolence" also does not fit. The search for the correct meaning is part of the process, and the discussion of what it can mean once the "evil" connotation is removed can be worthwhile.

The other psalms all had words that were problematic in the JPS translation. For instance, Ps. 27:5, "God will shelter me in God's pavilion" the Hebrew is *"sukkah"*. A *sukkah* (harvest hut) is a flimsy structure, while a pavilion sounds like a substantial building. Being sheltered in a pavilion sounds very significant but being sheltered in a *sukkah* leads to interesting work trying to understand the benefit of shelter in something that can blow over at any moment. The problem is that there is no good English word for *"sukkah"*.

References to God are mostly translated in gender-neutral terms: "The Holy One" or "God" instead of "He" or "the Lord." The Holy One is both genders, since humanity is a reflection of God's image. But for some people who never questioned God's male gender, the removal of the masculine references can be surprising, even disturbing. If you need gender-specific imagery for God, please feel free to designate the gender so you will be comfortable. It is not my intention to decide this for you, but simply to write in the way I am most comfortable describing the Holy One.

All translations are interpretive, including the translations used here. But using the original text in Hebrew is informative regarding the original intention of the psalmist. While there is validity to struggling with the words and their meanings in an English translation without reference to the original Hebrew, there are insights one would miss without the Hebrew. There are alliterations in the Hebrew where the sound and cadence of the words are important (e.g. Ps. 23, *lo ira ra*—'I will not be afraid of that which is bad.')

Interpretations of the Text

There are countless books written by people struggling to understand and interpret Biblical texts. This is an indication not only of the complexity of the process, and of the texts, but also an indication of the wisdom gleaned from many of them. Some interpretations make sense at one time in one's life, others at different times; some fit within one's religious beliefs, and some are contrary to those beliefs; some are bound by traditional understanding of the texts, and some overthrow those understandings.

For the purposes of this book, the interpretations are a mixture of traditional Jewish understanding of the text, heard but not studied over lifetimes, and insights which may have been gleaned from other sources. While these interpretations have meaning and "fit" for the authors, they are not more correct or "better" than other interpretations. They reflect our personal struggles to find meaning in the texts, yet do not reflect absolute answers. They are notes in a symphony of responses to the Biblical texts; few voices among many. Participants are welcome to question, disregard, reinterpret, disagree and respond in any other ways that fit for them; to add their voices to the symphony.

Psalms in the Key of Healing

Why Psalms?

According to Neil Gillman (2000), "Why Psalms? This image of God as refuge and protector, with the concomitant feeling of trust in God's power, is omnipresent in Psalms..." Gillman teaches that psalms were liturgical poems, written by more than one author. All of the authors expressed their own theologies while sharing a core set of beliefs. The tradition was "multi-vocal," attempting to express understanding of both the world and of God in a liturgical, poetic format.

This book is intended to enable us to engage in conversation with others about their theological understanding of the world and, when speaking with people living with illness, to converse about their illness itself, and help them in their struggle to find meaning, strength, and hope in the process. The methodology is, as suggested by Gillman (Gillman, p 76), "– to allow the psalm to speak to us, react to it, let the psalm elicit the feelings which are aroused by the psalm, and explore the psalmist's and our own theology through the words in the psalm. The psalm is a vehicle to the greater and deeper understanding of the self and one's theology."

Jews and Christians often refer to biblical texts, and use those texts as vehicles for teaching, sources of comfort, and expressions of understanding and challenge. Psalms, in particular, lend themselves well to study and liturgical use. But some psalms have also become closely associated with particular times and experiences. Psalm 23 is read at almost every funeral; Psalm 27 is recited traditionally by Jews during the High Holiday season; Psalm 121 is seen as a source of comfort for people who are struggling.

I presented Psalm 27 to an interfaith clergy group, mostly faith leaders from Harlem, New York. One of the people in the group was an imam. It was fascinating—he heard echoes from the psalm in the Qur'an. With each line, he was searching his holy book for the Muslim equivalent. There also was a Buddhist monk in the group. He also found ways of relating his religious background with the text. The themes are universal. All of us experience:

- *Perspective*
- *Grief*
- *Shame*
- *Mortality*
- *Trauma*
- *Growing Older*
- *Music of the Heart and Soul*
- *Forgiveness*
- *Hope and Joy*

I used to co-facilitate bereavement groups with a social worker. In working with bereavement groups, I used the Psalms as an opportunity to discuss theology as a component of the teaching agenda of these groups. While they seemed to, at times, derive comfort from the discussion of the Psalms, the goals of the program were a greater discussion of their personal beliefs about God, religion in their lives, their beliefs about the afterlife, and their effort to find perspective and meaning. But the use of the Psalms in this context had a positive impact on the participants. They gained perspective: they were not the only ones struggling with the issues raised in the Psalms. Psalms gave them a framework for asking themselves what they believe and how they saw God in the midst of their personal tragedies. Studying and responding to texts enabled the participants to rethink and express their theology as they reacted to the psalmist's theological struggles. Gillman continues:

> The language of poetry is never straightforward. It uses metaphor, allusion, and hyperbole; it suggests a feeling rather than conveying a message to teaching a lesson. That's why the use of a psalm as a theological statement is

doubly precarious. We can never get to that message directly. We have to begin by allowing the poem to speak to us, by coming into touch with our own feelings as we read the psalm, by letting out reactions to what the poet is saying seep into our consciousness. Our reaction may then guide us into the poet's feelings… therein lies the clue to the psalm's implicit theology (Gillman, p 76).

The challenge of understanding the poetry enables participants to focus their thoughts externally, to move from discussion of their experience of loss to discussion of the poetry. In some ways it normalizes their experiences of loss at the same time as it enables them to react to the text, to see the implications of their reactions in their bereavement. They discussed their experiences in a context of identifying with the feelings, emotions, and beliefs expressed in the psalm, even in disagreement with the text.

The book of Psalms is rich in spiritual concepts that have implications for healing, recovery, and journeying with illness. Readers will look at the text of the psalm, the overarching emotional theme of the psalm, the reaction each reader has with this concept in the text, for themselves, and implications of the text for other people in their lives.

Personal Theology

Speaking of theology, Rabbi Richard Address says:

Theology is about life's journey, both individual and collective. We become grounded as result of the journey which we walk. We believe we understand the journey and can articulate it in a way that makes sense. Sometimes, others

> want us to articulate our understanding of
> where they and we are on this journey... All
> theology is biography (Class on March 28,
> 2011).

Our understanding of theology is formed and expressed in personal experience of God, and life crises; loss and illness can be powerful opportunities for theological exploration.

The book of Psalms offers a basis for discussion of personal theology as it relates to the text. It is rich with opportunities for interpretation, reflection, and discussion. The psalms in this book offer a wide range of experience for examination and discussion, providing opportunities for greater self-awareness, open sharing, and enhanced self-confidence. Jews and Christians turn to the Bible, particularly Psalms, for strength, comfort, and hope. Using Psalms, one can clarify one's own spiritual, theological and religious perspectives, contrast one's perspectives with one's own background and with those of others, and incorporate sacred writings from other religions into further understanding of theology.

Readers from non-Jewish and non-Christian backgrounds may be interested in learning more in terms of actual content of religious texts so they can find points of agreement and divergence with their own faith traditions.

According to Abraham Joshua Heschel:

> There are three starting points to contemplation
> about God; three trails lead to Him. The first
> is the way of sensing the presence of God in
> the world, in things; the second is the way of
> sensing His presence in the Bible (e.g. Exodus
> 33:18); the third is the way of sensing His
> presence in sacred deeds (Heschel, 1955, 32.)

Psalms in the Key of Healing

The process of this book incorporates all three of these "starting points."

The in-depth study of Psalms is an opportunity to enhance our perspectives by exposing us to God's presence in the Bible, and the psalmist's perceptions of life's issues. Speaking with others and working through their theological concerns is the fulfillment of Heschel's third "starting point." Working with people who are ill, in emotional and/or spiritual crisis is holy work. The process invokes God's Presence.

Rabbi Harold Kushner describes the relationship with God this way:

> When I sit with a seriously ill patient in a hospital and pray with her, I explain that our prayer expresses our hopes for a favorable outcome. But more than that, I want the patient to know that she is ill not because God has rejected her or is punishing her for something. God is on her side, not on the side of the illness. God is sending her doctors and nurses, endowing them with skill and sensitivity. And even at night when the room is dark and deserted and she may feel desperately alone, she can call on God to keep her company. Asked by a television interviewer what I thought of an experiment that seemed to show that praying for people in hospitals made no difference, I told her, "God's job is not to make sick people healthy. That's the doctor's job. God's job is to make sick people brave" (Kushner, 2009, p 18.)

"Ritual makes sacred bridges from reality to holiness," according to Dr. Address (November 22, 2010). Using Psalms as a "starting point," they serve as the ritual described above, and provide that route to finding holiness.

Suffering and Divine Punishment

People struggle with suffering and a perception that illness is Divine punishment. Among the most common questions when a person is hospitalized are the "why" questions: Why me? Why now? Why this?. Illness as punishment from God for unknown (or assumed) sins or expression of guilt is commonplace among people who have not really explored their theology, and who are struggling to find some meaning in their illness. These psalms can help provide perspective, understanding of God as loving and compassionate, and the commonality of the human struggle to understand the Divine Will. Discussion of these psalms can help people draw their own conclusions about the nature of God in their lives, and how they can find meaning and hope in the midst of suffering.

"Everyone who has grappled with deep losses and experiences that threaten their physical and emotional well-being has faced the challenge of making sense of such suffering. People in crisis initially raise questions and make laments, like 'Why is this happening to me?' Their first attempts at answers come out of their embedded theology, out of the theological presuppositions that shape their lives and practices" (Doehring, 2006, 113).

The experience of people who are ill makes them most in need of a reconsideration of their embedded theology and they have an opportunity to develop a different understanding. Doehring proposes the following questions:

- Does her theology connect her with a compassionate loving God in moments when she condemns herself?
- Does his theology fully call him to account for the way in which he has hurt others?
- Does her theology keep her so focused on herself that she loses sight of the needs of others? Does it help her love her neighbor as

    herself?

- Does his theology help him live out the promises he made when he joined a community of faith?
- Does her theology help her apprehend the mystery of God's presence in the midst of her crisis?

These questions underpin some of these discussions of Psalms.

Overcoming Fear

Life is scary sometimes. Things you never expect become your reality, sometimes without warning. Illness can be scary, as can life without a loved one, or without a job, or without ___ (fill in the blank). The texts of the psalms in this book touch on issues of fear and confidence. The text in some ways normalizes the fear: if the author of the psalm can be afraid, and talk about his/her fears, we all can. Fear is part of our human experience.

We all have to confront our own fears and projections. Discussion of the psalmist's fears, and our own, can help us take steps to move beyond the fears which can paralyze us. And we can be afraid of saying the wrong things, saying too much, or not saying the right things. If we are the image of God, we have to accept that all of us, as that image, are approaching our understanding of theology together. There are no right or wrong answers; there is just the struggle to understand. Engagement in that process unifies us; the divergent answers, thoughts, and responses are equally valid. In the words of the Talmud, "Both this and this are the words of the Living God."

Process for Each Psalm

The best way to work through these psalms is with a study partner. While I know that's probably not how you usually read books, this one will be very difficult to really understand without dialogue. (Trust me: it's hard to write without dialogue!) The person you work with does not need to be more informed than you, or more learned, or even the same religion: s/he just needs to be someone you can talk to.

Here's your assignment:

1. Read the psalm in English and/or Hebrew, if you can.
2. Discuss what you think the psalm is about.
3. Reread the psalm in depth, pulling out specific words, sentences, and concepts that you find interesting.
4. Engage in the wording of the psalm: deep examination of the meaning and implications of the words of the text. To make the concept more accessible, equate the process to scuba diving, dive into it, as opposed to reading the text on the surface, like surfing.
5. What themes do you see beneath the surface of the psalm?
6. Relate the concepts to your own personal theology, world views, and cultural context.
7. Discuss the meaning of the psalm after deeper analysis of it. Examine the relationship between what it seemed to say on the surface and the deeper meanings elucidated through the closer reading of the text.
8. Consider the implications of this theme or theology for your own sense of meaning.
9. Define what has changed as a result of struggling with the words of this psalm.

If you're anything like me, you will look at the 9 instructions above, say "very nice," and read on. *Try to resist that temptation and find a partner.*

OK, so you are reading on anyway. Try to remember that you are not reading the "Right Answers," and that our perspectives are just that. Once you read through these psalms on your own, consider going back and discussing with a partner.

My Diagnosis

I was with my best friend on a cruise and turned incredibly itchy and yellow. We got off the ship and went to Urgent Care in the Grand Cayman Islands. They said I had hepatitis, not A, B, or C. They said I should go to a hospital, but the ship was about to leave, so we got off the next day at the next port. The Emergency Room doctor in Cozumel said "You probably won't die today unless you get hit by a bus" so I should go home to an emergency room my insurance would cover. The ER doctor there ordered a CT scan and other tests and then said, "This is how pancreatic cancer usually presents."

The GI doctor the next day said it was more likely bile duct cancer. He put a stent in my bile duct to get it working and get rid of the yellow and itching. My brother flew to Miami from Philadelphia, and my sister and brother-in-law flew in from New Jersey. My brother and I met with the oncologist, who ordered more tests.

Bile duct cancer is hard to find. So, they decided to look for metastases of the cancer in nodules in my lungs. The biopsy showed that I had lung cancer, in addition to whatever was happening in my bile duct. Both cancers are adenocarcinomas, so both would get the same treatment: chemotherapy. I got off the ship on March 14, 2019 and started chemo, after months of unclear diagnoses, on July 24, 2019. I am writing this at the end of October, 2020.

Chemo has been no picnic. I have wondered whether the cure was worse than the disease. I am very grateful for the family, professionals, and friends who have kept me alive through this illness. I am hoping to live long enough to see this book in print and sign some copies.

Writing this book has been a blessing for me. Working through these psalms again and again, has brought me closer to understanding my place in God's flock (Psalm 23) to better self acceptance (Psalm 27) to living with my own mortality (Psalm 91) to letting go of bitterness and anger (Psalm 103) having hope (Psalm 121) and gratitude (Psalm 150). I am very grateful to the Holy One who has sustained me, kept me alive, and enabled me to reach this moment.

— H.R.G.

Rabbi Goldstein died on December 21st, 2020.

— The Publisher

Psalm 1

Finding Perspective, Moving Forward

Translation and Interpretation by
Rabbi Dr. J.B. Sacks

The visitor to the zoo was passing the elephants and suddenly stopped, confused by the fact that these huge creatures were being held by only a small rope tied to their front leg. No chains, no cages. It was obvious that the elephants could, at any time, break away from their bonds but for some reason, they did not.

The visitor saw a trainer nearby and asked why these animals just stood there and made no attempt to get away. "Well," the trainer answered, "when they were very young and much smaller we used the same size rope to tie them and, at that age, it's enough to hold them. As they grow up, they are conditioned to believe they cannot break away. They believe the rope can still hold them, so they never try to break free."

The visitor was amazed. These animals could at any time break free from their bonds but because they believed they couldn't, they were stuck right where they were.

31

Psalms in the Key of Healing

This story resonates with me. Sometimes we feel stuck in life. We have been hit hard by life and its challenges. Our health may not seem to be improving, or, indeed, is not. Our job does not seem to be leading anywhere. We might be in a relationship, but wonder if, after all these years, we are still in love. There are so many roadblocks that we find in life, and all it takes is one to stop us in our life tracks.

We can be like the elephants, living as if we are all tied up, bound by a limited number of choices and restricted by our circumstances. It does feel that way sometimes. And, like the elephants, we sometimes continue living inside this paradigm long after it's necessary and long after it's healthful for us to do so.

Even elephants, I guess, sometimes ignore the elephant in the room! So, how do we regain our balance, our perspective, our vision when we need it most? Can we move forward? If so, when? And how?

Giving us the inspiration to know we have the wherewithal to move forward is, to me, the purpose of the very first psalm in the Bible. It tries to both prevent us who are not currently camped by a roadblock to avoid doing so, and it helps others regain their wherewithal to move forward.

Here is my translation:

1 Moving forward is the person who has not
    walked with the advice of the wayward,
    nor stood on the road of the strayers,
    nor sat in the seat of the scoffers.
2 Rather, in HaShem's guidance: their delight;
    and on that guidance
    does such a person cogitate constantly.
3 Such a person shall be like
    a tree planted over streams of water,
    that yields its fruit in due season,

and whose leaves don't wither:
in all ways,
always advancing.
4 Not so the wayward; rather,
they are like chaff,
which the wind whisks about.
5 Therefore the wayward one
cannot rise in rectitude,
nor can the strayers
in the congregation of the righteous.
6 For HaShem indicates the way of the righteous;
the wayward's way: lost.

אַשְׁרֵי־הָאִישׁ אֲשֶׁר | לֹא הָלַךְ בַּעֲצַת רְשָׁעִים
וּבְדֶרֶךְ חַטָּאִים לֹא עָמָד וּבְמוֹשַׁב לֵצִים לֹא יָשָׁב:
כִּי אִם בְּתוֹרַת יְהֹוָה חֶפְצוֹ וּבְתוֹרָתוֹ יֶהְגֶּה יוֹמָם וָלָיְלָה:
וְהָיָה כְּעֵץ שָׁתוּל עַל־פַּלְגֵי מָיִם אֲשֶׁר פִּרְיוֹ |
יִתֵּן בְּעִתּוֹ וְעָלֵהוּ לֹא־יִבּוֹל וְכֹל אֲשֶׁר־יַעֲשֶׂה יַצְלִיחַ:
לֹא־כֵן הָרְשָׁעִים כִּי אִם־כַּמֹּץ אֲשֶׁר־תִּדְּפֶנּוּ רוּחַ:
עַל־כֵּן | לֹא־יָקֻמוּ רְשָׁעִים בַּמִּשְׁפָּט וְחַטָּאִים בַּעֲדַת צַדִּיקִים:
כִּי־יוֹדֵעַ יְהֹוָה דֶּרֶךְ צַדִּיקִים וְדֶרֶךְ רְשָׁעִים תֹּאבֵד:

This psalm, we might first notice, feels like a short poem that
is all about movement. It begins by reminding us that to move
forward we must avoid certain things, and it ends by reminding
us that God helps us by pointing out our path to us. The psalmist
is so committed to each person's potential to get beyond where
they feel stuck now, and is so fully committed to our future, that
we gain more confidence and hope in ourselves, our potential,
our future, and in life every time we reflect on this psalm.

Moving Forward—Ashrei

"Moving forward" is my translation of the first word of

the psalm—*ashrei* (pronounced *osh-ray*). The word appears fairly often in the book of Psalms, some 26 times (out of 45 total occurrences in the Hebrew Bible). The Hebrew alphabet also served as a numerical system (and still does today in the modern state of Israel). The most intimate name for God in the Bible is rendered by the letters YHVH, whose numerical values add up to 26 as well. So, from a Jewish spiritual perspective, our lives move forward when we live with an awareness of God's Presence. By mentioning *ashrei* 26 times throughout the psalms, the book keeps reminding us that wherever we are, we are not stuck: we can move forward.

Standard translations for *ashrei* use "blessed," "praised," or "happy." These translations point to feelings that a person might have or something that others, especially God, might do for us. This psalm, however, is not about feelings or what others might do. Rather, this psalm of movement is about our possibilities of doing, going, of regaining control over ourselves so that we can move forward.

If the psalmist wanted to say "blessed" or "praised," then the psalmist would have used the word *baruh* (blessed), or *hullal* (praised). *Baruh* is the first word of every standard Jewish blessing; *hullal* is related to *Halleluyah*, literally meaning "Praise the Holy One," or its English equivalent, "Hallelujah." Hebrew readers know that *ashrei* cannot mean "blessed" or "praised." The word "happy," can mean a number of things, especially "characterized by good luck," "enjoying pleasure," and "felicitous." These meanings suggest something temporary or ephemeral. The psalmist, however, is not speaking about happenstance, or luck, or something coincidental or random.

Rather, the psalmist is offering an approach to life that can keep us on track and in the right direction. We need to flourish without regard to luck, and we can't let the hope of good luck or the fear of bad luck be what primarily determines our lives. We can and must make good decisions for ourselves and move forward. Life does challenge and hurt us, but it makes no sense to remain in a rut indefinitely—or to wait until we feel sure that fate will be kind. Rather, when we start to figure out our path and to walk on it, the hurt and pain that our inertia exacerbated begins to go away, and we start to feel more confident, healthier of spirit, and something that is more of a deeper satisfaction than the momentary "happy." Therefore, the psalmist uses the word *ashrei*, derived from a root meaning, "to walk" or "to move."

In Psalms, *ashrei* refers to the eventual attainment of all that is desirable. This may be an elusive goal and, perhaps, a shifting goal, especially as the events of our lives unfold, and the facts of our lives on the ground continue to affect how we frame and chart our destiny. Nonetheless, it sure is comforting to me to know that this is possible. The things that I hope for in life— love, honor, family, whatever—are not merely my dreams. They can actually be mine. Psalm 1 holds this up for us to see.

The hopes and dreams we have for ourselves can only happen, however, when we take steps to realize them. *Ashrei* signifies movement that is intentional, moving towards both the vision we have for our lives and the goals that we set to help us better realize that vision and become one with it. *Ashrei*, then, points to an essentially dynamic concept, a sense of someone in process—perhaps currently in a rut—but someone striving to move forward in their life.

Ashrei also has something to do with being in right relationship with the Holy One, with God. The book of Psalms depicts someone who is *ashrei* as "walking on the Holy One's path" (Psalm 119:1) and as "revering the Holy One" (Psalm 128:1). Nonetheless, the psalmist's focus is that the key to flourishing in our lives is to move forward. That message matters no matter what someone believes in God—or even *if* they believe in God.

The word *ashrei*, it is good to keep in mind, inaugurates the entire book of Psalms. This word serves as the gateway into the world of psalms. To enter this world, one must be searching for a life that "is striding forward," the ever-striving life, the life of spiritual depth, the life of oneness with God and the universe but one that remains, nevertheless, dynamic

Everyone may aspire to the ascription of a life that is *ashrei*. Otherwise, the psalmist would use another term; this psalm would not open the entire book. We can live a life that is *ashrei*, no matter what we must confront in our lives. But while we can both be *ashrei*, we each must become so in our own way—we must each forge our own path to become *ashrei*. There are many paths, but there will only be one that is really mine, and only one that will be truly yours.

It seems important to note that the word *ashrei* is plural, yet it is clearly applied here to a single individual, the psalmist. This is always the case. Even in those cases where *ashrei* is applied to a people, the word for people is also a singular term. What lessons might using a plural term for a single individual teach us?

First, such usage may intend to encompass each individual. We cannot read the psalm and think, "Oh, that's not me," or "I can't become like that," or—whatever our "or" is at the moment. The book of Psalms, however, is universal and applies to everyone. So, at such times, we should remind ourselves that we all live in relationships, and we honor those relationships precisely by listening to those who love us and care about us. The word *ashrei*, in plural form, reminds us that we grow and move forward, in great part, because of these relationships and circles of friendships.

The second lesson of *ashrei* being in a plural form is to remind us that no one grows constantly, just as no one grows only at one time or in one single moment of one's life. People move forward many times and continuously throughout life.

"not walked with the advice of the wayward..."

So, how do we move forward? Sometimes we are so confused or befuddled that we are not sure how to move forward.

Sometimes we are too fearful or scared to do so. Sometimes we are beside ourselves with loss or rage. It can be difficult to move forward.

The psalmist begins, then, by offering something sensible: Clear out of the way the things you can. Some things are obviously not helpful or healthful—put them aside.

To do this, the psalmist offers three things to avoid. The first suggestion is not to walk in the counsel of the wayward. Some translations have "counsel" rather than "advice." I chose "advice," however, because sometimes "counsel" sounds very specific, like a technical advice, such as when we speak of "legal counsel." I don't think the psalmist has in mind only, or even primarily, that kind of advice.

Most likely we feel something inside physically when someone offers us advice that we know we should not even consider at the moment, but sometimes we feel too weak and so give in and heed that advice. While many times this is understandable, it is never optimal. Moving forward blindly or precipitously is not moving forward with "God's guidance."

The psalmist here calls persons who offer such advice *r'sha'im*, which I translate as "wayward." Most often this term is translated as "wicked," but "wicked" often sounds judgmental, whether in Hebrew or English. I am not in the business of judging people, nor do I think we should get in the habit of name-calling. It's hard to think of a single benefit to using the language of judgment or dislike.

The psalmist pictures good and righteous people as few, and the *r'sha'im* as many. Most of us, however, are not "wicked" or "evil." Rather, we are the many, trying to refine our rough edges and gather the reins of our lives. And so, too, are the majority of people who offer advice, good and not-so-good.

When the Bible uses *rasha* (singular of *r'sha'im*), it is coming from the point of view of an ancient Semitic cognate root that means "ill-regulated." Many people cannot regulate themselves—they have poor boundaries, or poor filters, or do not (or cannot) exhibit good judgment, or do not think through the consequences of the advice they are about to offer, or have not actually been geared to think ethically, or they have some combination of these. When someone exhibits any of these characteristics, they are acting in a way that the psalmist would call *rasha*.

When the Bible calls someone a *rasha*, it is not necessarily doing so as a moral judgment. It is sometimes merely being descriptive. The psalmist seems to know that the distance between a "righteous" person and a "wicked" person is the distance it takes for us to nod our head "yes" once to a bad piece of advice. This can be you or me. No one is immune. Therefore, we need a less dramatic, and less judgmental, term. "Ill-regulated" is mine.

Why Wayward?

First and foremost, the word, at its core, means "turning away." In a psalm about movement, and moving forward, it seems fitting that the first suggestion is that we be careful not to turn away or aside from our own path, our own truths, or our own way. The word "wayward" often means "turning away from what is right or proper," and that meaning starts to hone in on what the psalmist seems to care about: the choices we must make and the actions we must take to move forward and get the most out of our lives.

The word "wayward" can also mean "prompted or swayed by caprice." Who knows why we might give or take ill-considered advice? Yes, fear or other things are sometimes present, but we don't always make bad decisions at such times. There is a certain amount of "caprice" or arbitrariness to our yielding to the advice of others, even against our own intuition and better judgment.

Finally, "wayward" can mean "irregular," and this gets to the notion that those who give such advice are (at least, at the moment), "ill-regulated." That, to me, is a good way of framing this. But equally so, when we take someone else's ill-given advice on the spot without due consideration, then we too, at that moment, show ill-regulation. This is what the psalmist wishes us to avoid.

The first piece of advice from the psalmist, then, is not to follow the advice of those who are wayward. So when we dare to give advice, we must be exceedingly cautious to ensure that we are well-regulated at the moment, and have thought through the possibilities and their consequences, because someone just might take our advice. And that person definitely will have to live with the consequences, not us. And it is always good to keep in mind that we cannot undo the giving of advice to someone who has just acted upon it. This kind of self-regulation is best served with caution and humility, which are not hallmarks of the ill-regulated.

How might we avoid bad advice? For starters, when someone is offering advice at a bad time, we should find a way to say, "Now is not a good time." A second way to avoid bad advice is to "check the math." Sometimes the good decisions of others would not be good decisions for you. Make sure that what someone is saying actually will work for you.

"not walked with the advice..."

Both the Jewish Publication Society and the New Revised Standard Version use the term "followed." Following advice is the usual English expression, and so both versions convey the essence. The Hebrew, however, clearly has "walk," not "follow." Following advice can sound like a "one-and-done" matter. But by using the word "walk," the psalmist is suggesting that while we might listen to someone's advice, we don't have to take it. If it sounds good, we still should check it out. Here the psalmist suggests that the following of ill-regulated advice can diminish us, for each of us must live with the afterlife of any advice we take.

Sometimes when we are weak or feeling vulnerable, we are apt to yield our power for maintaining our lives. We become prone to seek out the help of others. But we should not confuse advice with solutions. It is up to us to "check the math."

"nor stood on the road of the strayers..."

The second characteristic of those who are *ashrei* is that they do not stand on the road of the strayers. Most translations call these people "sinners," not "strayers." My objection here about the word "sinners" being judgmental applies as much as it did when translators used "wicked" for *rasha*.

The Hebrew word used is ⬛*ata'im*. Here, however, the word is definitely not used as a moral judgment against the person. The Hebrew root means "to miss the mark" or "to fail to find," and can also mean "to commit a mistake or error." None of these meanings imply judgment, only missteps. Of course, missing the mark or committing a mistake is not the ideal, but it is also not anyone's intention.

I sense a tendency in our culture to demonize too many people far too quickly for far too little. Words can really hurt. The psalmist here is not trying to hurt or demonize but merely explain a common tendency and hope we avoid it.

The word "strayers" is a better term, even if it is not a word we commonly use. The English word "to stray" means "to deviate from the direct course, leave the proper place, or go beyond the proper limits, especially without a fixed course or purpose; ramble." Sometimes we recognize that someone else is going in a bad direction. They are *hata'im*. They are not "bad" people. We would rather they not go down an unproductive path; the psalmist recommends that we not join them.

"nor sat in the seat of the scoffers..."

JPS calls these people "insolent." Insolent people are "boldly rude or disrespectful." They will do things and say things to get a negative reaction, and they will do so in an offensive way. They want you to dislike them. Scoffers are also often unpleasant, but they are not insolent. Rather, they "mock, jeer, and deride." These people are cynical, and they will belittle every idea and every positive posture you or I make. Scoffers infect our world with negativity. The psalmist is not telling us to avoid being rude; rather, we should not become scoffers, or people who put out negativity regularly.

This now makes "sat in the seat" the precise words of the psalmist. JPS renders this part as "joined the company." The Hebrew "sat in one's seat," however, suggests that "I have become like that person." Someone who sits in the seat of scoffers has themselves become a scoffer. That in fact seems the intention of the ambiguous term "sit," for the Hebrew word *yashav*, in the Bible, means not only "to sit," but also "to dwell," "to stay," or "to endure."

Walked... Stood... Sat

In this psalm of movement, the psalmist lists three things that a person who is *ashrei* will avoid in order to keep a proper frame. Note, however, that the number three is probably symbolic. Three is the smallest number to form a chain, and chains are endless. Therefore, when the psalmist offers three suggestions, that should signal to us, "O.K. three—and probably more." There are any number of ways we sabotage ourselves or otherwise find ourselves not where we should be in our lives. The psalmist lists some common ones.

The psalmist's three things are placed purposefully, to represent a descending order of experience. The person who is *ashrei* avoids "walking with the advice of the wayward"—taking ill-considered advice and living in light of that advice.

Spiritually lower, however, is the person "stands on the road of the strayers"—the one who veers off their own life course onto someone else's, realizes it, and remains frozen, not wanting to go down that road, but not knowing how to turn around. The strayers on this path cannot offer us any true support. After all, they are not situated in a healthy place. This person needs to retrace their steps to get back on their own life track.

Spiritually lower yet are those who "sit in the seat of the scoffers"—those who have completely taken on a constantly negative profile, and continually doubt how precious and worthwhile life itself is. It will be more difficult for a negative person to even feel there's a reason to care about their own path.

"Rather, in HaShem's guidance: their delight..."

The Hebrew word that I have rendered as "guidance" is *torah* and I have purposefully spelled it without capitalizing it. For contemporary Jews, the word *Torah* usually refers to the first five books of the Bible, written on a scroll and read from regularly in ritual settings. It is natural, then, for Jews to see the word *torah* in this light. Nonetheless, the word *torah* rarely, if ever, refers in the Hebrew Bible to any notion of such a five-book collection.

JPS renders the word *torah* as "teaching." A teaching is something very specific, and often something that originates from the teacher and holds out an answer that resides in the teacher. A teaching may or may not matter, or be relevant, to the recipient. The psalmist, however, clearly has a larger notion in mind, something that could help someone move forward in their life.

So How Did I Come to "Guidance?"

The word "*torah*" comes from a verb, *yarah*, which in its basic form means "to shoot." It is often used for shooting arrows. The same root is used in modern Hebrew. But this brings up the question: What does the Torah have in common with shooting arrows? What connects them? For me, it is the idea of aiming. The Torah is used to help us find our aim in life, enabling us to aim high. It follows that when the Bible uses the word *torah*, it refers to something that helps us to look forward in our lives, anything that helps remind us of our journey—where we say we want to go. Anything that helps us in such a way is "torah." Thus we can think of *torah* as something that mentors us; that guides us.

I have chosen to use HaShem as a translation for the specific name of God in this passage and used later on here. That name of God is related to "existence" or "being." That name of God is so holy that Jews traditionally only pronounce it in appropriate situations, like prayer. HaShem literally means "the Name," but it is used as a term of endearment for God.

In Psalm 1, the psalmist finds delight in God's guidance. The psalmist has an evolved soul, is deeply attuned to life, emotionally vital, and growing spiritually. Therefore, paying attention to signs from God, looking for wisdom in nature, in one's own experience, or in sacred texts, are all ways to meet God and to find guidance.

The starting point of guidance is always the one who is trying to help another. Guidance as wisdom and direction is imparted in the hopes of affecting that person positively. However, it is always the recipient who must manage, assess, synthesize, and integrate such ideas into their lives. In Psalm 1, clearly God's *torah*, God's guidance, is meant to help the psalmist, who is deeply considering that *torah*. It is most often subtle: an intuition, a "still small voice," a possibility, or an insight. It is we who must take Divine guidance and shape it appropriately for our own context and our own lives.

Guidance from anyone, even from God, must be filtered by each of us and shaped. We often know inside what is best for us. That's not always, or even usually, the problem. Most often, a person with a substance abuse disorder knows that getting off that substance is imperative to their functioning and well-being; agoraphobes know they need to leave the house; workaholics, deep down, know that every evening ends in a sunset — and that the cost of missing five (or more) of them a week is quite dear.

43

Yes, the psalmist understands that knowledge, counsel, and wisdom are not enough. It is the psalmist's own life path, and the psalmist who must choose when to step and where to go. Each of us, like the psalmist, has our own journey to make. No one, not even God, can make the choice to act for us.

"and on that guidance
does such a person cogitate constantly..."

Sometimes it takes discernment to figure out what is what. A forward-seeking person is also one who reflects. That is why the psalmist "cogitates" continuously. The word "cogitate" means "to think hard about, to ponder, to meditate." This is precisely what the psalmist is recommending for the forward-striving person. The Hebrew root can literally mean "to moan" or "to mutter," meaning that the experience and guidance of God affects us in a visceral way, and that we not just reflect on our lives, but that we process intentionally our experience and life lessons; we "talk through" what's on our mind. Verbalizing sometimes, even to ourselves, is often a healthful component of "pondering" or "meditating" on our lives.

JPS uses "studies," probably because they translated *torah* as "teaching." But that's not what the Hebrew states — the idea of study is too narrow of a concept for the lofty goal of life-management.

Finally, I have suggested in my translation that the psalmist commends doing such "cogitation" constantly. The Hebrew means "day and night," and both JPS and the NRSV translate it literally. The psalmist wants us to meditate, reflect, do a "deep dive," on a regular basis.

"Such a person shall be like a tree..."

The psalmist in verse 1 tells us what the forward-striving person avoids doing and, worse, avoids becoming. In verse 2 the psalmist tells us what that person does, what is indicative of that person.

Now, in verse 3 the psalmist describes what such a person is like. The psalmist first lets us know that such a person might be compared to a tree. So, let us ask: how are trees like people?

- No two trees and no two people are alike. All vary in height, volume, color, etc.
- Both trees and people are built to stand upright and proud.
- Both rely on others for survival and proper functioning.
- Both are communal organisms that not only work with members of their own sphere but can form alliances with those outside.
- Both seek the light.

Any combination of these ideas, perhaps all, may be embedded in the choice of the psalmist to compare the forward-striving person to a tree.

"...planted over streams of water..."

The JPS and NRSV translations use "by," which makes good sense in English. The word in biblical Hebrew for "by" or "beside" is not *al* but, rather, *eitzel*. The Hebrew word *al*, however, means "upon" or "on," hence "over."

What might this cultural choice of the word "over" mean or teach us here? The first thing I sense is that trees over water have a generous and constant source of nourishment. The forward-striving person must also get continuously nourished from many people and from many places.

Learning from many people and places can be complicated, especially when different information appears contradictory, even mutually exclusive. This comes in with the word "streams." The Hebrew word *peleg* comes from the root meaning "to split" or "to divide."

When I read the Psalm, I picture a tree over an intersection of two or more streams. They are distinct and have their own direction, their own course. When we hear from others, we help ourselves avoid the pitfalls that might mark the ill-regulated. We have to stand above the conflicts and the agendas of others. In doing this, we can make the best choices for ourselves to move forward.

"that yields its fruit in due season, and whose leaves don't wither..."

That a tree produces fruit suggests that a tree is not just about the tree. The tree, as part of a biosphere, gives to others. So, too, when we are at our best, we do not just live an interior life; rather, we are interdependent with our sphere, both the people who inhabit it and the land which is part of it.

That the tree's leaves do not wither suggests its ongoing vitality. So too, when we are functioning well, we remain vital. Remaining vital does not mean we feel great every day, experience a lack of problems, or stay forever young, just as having leaves in good condition does not necessarily tell you about another part of the tree, about the biosphere which it inhabits, or that the tree is in its youth or "prime." At any age a hardy tree has vital leaves. This, in fact, is our ongoing possibility: that no matter what is going on, and no matter our age, we have the potential to live vital lives.

In using the metaphor of a tree, the psalmist gives a picture of what a flourishing life looks and feels like, whether it is a tree—or us.

"...in all ways, always advancing..."

JPS takes this as applying to the tree and translates this as "whatever it produces thrives." The NRSV, on the other hand, understands this as descriptive of *ashrei* people who resemble trees, and renders this as "in all that they do, they prosper." The problem is that both translations choose one possibility over the other, without considering that the psalmist may have meant both the tree and the person who resembles it. My translation retains the ambiguity, so that we can understand it as referring to both.

For the last part of the sentence, the NRSV uses "prospers," but to me that conjures up the idea of external flourishing and not necessarily internal. JPS translates as "thrives," but strangely applies this to the fruit of the tree, not to the health and well-being of the tree itself. However, the psalm is talking about our core being, and uses the tree as a metaphor. The psalmist is concerned about us, not about the well-being of the fruit of our labors.

The root of the Hebrew word means "to advance" and in keeping with a psalm of movement, the choice seems purposeful. A person who is *ashrei*, who is forward-striving, is always advancing. In fact, they are "in all ways, always advancing." In all ways, because the flourishing and advancement is both internal and external.

"Not so the wayward; rather, they are like chaff, which the wind whisks away..."

In the first three verses, the psalmist laid out an understanding of the world, and a hope for all of us. Flourishing, self-actualized people are characterized as *ashrei*—forward-striving. The first two verses tell us what the *ashrei* person avoids and what an *ashrei* person does, respectively. The third verse builds on this by employing the image of a tree to describe who that person is, what they feel, and how they function.

Now the psalmist in this fourth verse, asks us to consider the alternative—the *rasha*—the ill-regulated. The psalmist also uses an image culled from nature: the chaff of a plant, dispersed by the wind. This is stark imagery. Chaff refers to the light outer side of the husk of a grain. This part is separated from the grain during threshing; it is unusable. Because the grain is what the user wants and prizes, and not the chaff, which is discarded, the word "chaff" is synonymous with "worthless matter; refuse."

The chaff does not weigh much and is inconsequential. It is easily driven about by the wind, and it leaves no impression behind. The kind of wind that drives chaff about is one that is strong and swirling. The chaff does not go merely in one direction at one speed to some endpoint. Rather, it gets whisked up and keeps changing direction as the gusts of wind change.

Unregulated people, in this imagery, are like the chaff, who are not grounded and without vision. They have movement, but it is not conducted by them or on their terms. Rather, life blows them around, and they land where they land. They are too busy managing the falls and the rides in between to build a legacy that expresses their core being. Like chaff, they are largely absent from familial and communal engagement, and so leave no positive, lasting mark. They are there, briefly, then they are gone.

The verb used here is *nadaf*, meaning "to drive about." It connotes an ongoing sense of being driven; the being driven has no control. Here chaff has no control over itself, and it is not driven with any particular purpose or goal in mind.

The psalmist wants us to ward off this kind of life, before we develop habits, postures, or processes that cause our lives to languish. Our psalmist knows that this does not have to be; it is not determined or inevitable. Even the ill-regulated are never described as being chaff, rather, merely *like* chaff. This is an important distinction, because at every step of the way, at any moment of time, we might once again, like a tree, stand tall and proud. We can realize that our leaves remain vital, that we can regain our vision, find our path, and step forward. It does take the fortitude and tenacity of a tree, but we are more like a tree than perhaps anything else. We can endure, and we can thrive. We can matter.

"*Therefore the wayward one cannot rise in rectitude...*"

My rendering here is admittedly unusual. JPS understands this as "the wicked will not survive judgment." However, the verb they render as "survive" is *kum*, which means "to rise" or "to stand." This psalm suggests that God holds out guidance, even a lure, for people to take the necessary and best steps for themselves. The psalm does not speak of God rendering judgments.

Further, the psalm is not concerned about what someone may or may not face, and it does not contemplate anyone's fate. Rather, it is only concerned about those who have a life—and plenty of it—ahead of them.

The noun *mishpat* can mean "judgment," as JPS translates. However, it also refers to the attribute of the one who judges, governs, or chooses. As such it can mean "rightness" or "rectitude." I chose "rectitude" because this word, to me, encompasses integrity and sound judgment, and can refer to both a person's character and being. We await and reflect upon God's subtle yet loving guidance in our lives—and that enables us to become *ashrei*, to move forward.

When the psalmist claims that the ill-regulated cannot rise up in *mishpat*, they are not able to regulate themselves often enough to live in rectitude, or to be right with themselves and right with God. They will make poor decisions more often, and not stay true to themselves, more often finding themselves posturing rather than living authentically (and more often lack the discernment to make good decisions for themselves). Again, this is not a judgment—it is a description. Perhaps they might get themselves better regulated. Perhaps they will get a "God shot" and re-track themselves. Perhaps those who are *ashrei* will give "fruit in due season," helping to get the ill-regulated onto a path that will lead to better self-regulation and to moving forward in their lives.

"...nor can the strayers in the congregation of the righteous..."

In a parallel way, those who have strayed from their authentic path often have a hard time integrating into communities. Perhaps some are ashamed. Perhaps they do not really know who they are and, therefore, do not know where or how to fit in. They may therefore self-isolate and avoid social situations.

Hence the text does not just state "the congregation," which otherwise would suffice, but "the congregation of the righteous." When someone judges themselves negatively, they tend to think that everyone else is righteous, better than they are, or more worthy than they are.

The psalmist, however, does not judge — the psalmist explains. And we need not judge ourselves against others, we merely need to move forward.

"For HaShem indicates the way of the righteous..."

In this final verse, the psalmist gives a concluding statement, succinctly restating the basic idea underlying this psalm. The word "indicates" renders the Hebrew word *yada*, which basically means "knows." It's a problem for every translator, since clearly the point is not that God "knows" the way of the righteous. That does not tell us anything we don't already know. Besides, doesn't God also "know" the way of the ill-regulated?

But why "indicate?" The psalmist's point has to do with how the *ashrei* (the forward-moving) person appropriates God's guidance. The sense of looking for, struggling with, assessing, and acting on God's guidance suggests that God "indicates," and we take those cues and shape them into our beings, so that we can move forward in the best way and flourish in our lives.

"...the wayward's way: lost..."

Rather than "lost," the NRSV uses "perish," a possible

translation, while JPS uses "doomed." However, do "ways" or "paths" perish? Are they "doomed?" The Hebrew means "lost." In 1 Samuel 9:3, for example, the donkeys belonging to Kish, King Saul's father, are "lost" for three days and then were found alive. Clearly the word cannot mean "perished" or "died," since the donkeys were found alive.

This translation is strengthened by the entire context of the psalm. In it, the psalmist speaks of moving forward on one's path, and how ill-regulated people have more difficulty doing this more often than those who are forward-striving. But people who walk uncharted paths do get "lost," at least for a time. In fact, when referring to people, we assume that the state of being lost is an impermanent one, and that the lost person will either be found by someone—or find their own way. We use the expression "to lose one's way" metaphorically as well. Again, it has the underlying sense that this is impermanent.

This matters. We all can experience a lack of control, or an ill-regulated time in our lives when we might feel lost. But we can all get back on track, with the guidance of God, with the help of others, and with our own efforts. Quite often, these three work in concert with each other.

Pulling It All Together

Psalm 1 offers a brief, uncomplicated view of life. First it gives us a vision. We should always keep our sights on what's important in life, what our dreams are, what the larger picture is. At the same time the psalm keeps us grounded—it knows that we have to take up our individual journeys step by step, and that along the way we might be tempted or cajoled to get off from our path and onto someone else's.

Being grounded is important. If we have our head in the clouds and are drifting in the wind, then it is hard to create consistent success for ourselves. The psalmist knows that we need to plant our feet firmly in the earth and stretch our head to the clouds so that we can bring our dreams into reality, or at least give ourselves the opportunity to do so.

Finally, and most important, we learn from this psalm that we must balance the vision and the lofty, larger view of our lives, with the need to live, work, breathe, play, and love each other every day.

For this, I look to the biblical figure of Moses as a model and teacher, particularly the story of him and the Israelite people gathered at Mount Sinai. The people were at the foot of the mountain; Moses stood on the peak. I learn from this image that Moses was a magnificent leader because he saw with Sinai vision even after he descended from the mountain. He didn't stay at the top of the mountain, and he did not forget about it when he came down. Rather, he integrated his vision, his dreams, and his goals with every step on the path through the wilderness toward his (and the people's), Promised Land. He may not have entered, but that matters little to anyone. His was a meaningful, rich, and model life.

Some people never seem to see the view from the top of the mountain; others climb to the top of the mountain but never seem to take in the view. They are too busy admiring their climb (See Psalm 121). Still others come down from the mountain and quickly forget the vision they obtained there. Moses, however, was like the artist, who can take in both the long view of his horizon as well as the knowledge of his own location, reality, and experience—and then integrate both views.

We, too, can shift our perspective by carrying this image with us. Perspective is, after all, that character strength that enables us to see both landscape and foreground; the forest and the trees. With perspective we are able to avoid staring at the leaves on a tree when there are bigger concerns we must confront. Perspective helps us to think about life's lessons and what's the best option for action at the moment. Perspective is getting that snapshot from Mount Sinai, having a *kodesh* moment—a moment of clarity, inspiration, and revelation—and then living accordingly.

From this perspective, Psalm 1 is a vehicle to help us remember and regain our vision, to make sure of our moorings, and to motivate us to move forward, while keeping a perspective that both holds out our vision of life and keep us grounded in it at the same time. When that happens, we become *ashrei*. That is our hope. That is our challenge. And, I pray, that is our blessing.

Psalm 23

Grief

Translation and Interpretation by
Rabbi Dr. Rafael Goldstein, BCC

A Psalm of David
1. The Holy One is my shepherd;
   I will not be overlooked.
2. God makes me lie down in green pastures;
   God leads me beside still waters.
3. God renews my life.
   God guides me in circles of justice
   as befits God's name.
4. Though I walk through the valley
   of the shadow of death,
   I will not be afraid of anything
   for You are with me.
   Your rod and Your staff comfort me.
5. You spread a table before me in full view of my enemies.
   You anoint my head with oil;
   my cup is overflowing.

6. Only goodness and steadfast love

    will pursue me all the days of my life,

    and I will dwell in the house of the Holy One forever.

מִזְמוֹר לְדָוִד יְהוָה רֹעִי לֹא אֶחְסָר׃

בִּנְאוֹת דֶּשֶׁא יַרְבִּיצֵנִי עַל־מֵי מְנֻחוֹת יְנַהֲלֵנִי׃

נַפְשִׁי יְשׁוֹבֵב יַנְחֵנִי בְמַעְגְּלֵי־צֶדֶק לְמַעַן שְׁמוֹ׃

גַּם כִּי־אֵלֵךְ בְּגֵיא צַלְמָוֶת לֹא־אִירָא רָע כִּי־אַתָּה עִמָּדִי

שִׁבְטְךָ וּמִשְׁעַנְתֶּךָ הֵמָּה יְנַחֲמֻנִי׃

תַּעֲרֹךְ לְפָנַי ׀ שֻׁלְחָן נֶגֶד צֹרְרָי דִּשַּׁנְתָּ בַשֶּׁמֶן רֹאשִׁי כּוֹסִי רְוָיָה׃

אַךְ ׀ טוֹב וָחֶסֶד יִרְדְּפוּנִי כָּל־יְמֵי חַיָּי וְשַׁבְתִּי בְּבֵית־יְהוָה לְאֹרֶךְ יָמִים׃

Psalm 23 is probably, on the surface, the best known of the psalms. It has become associated with death, loss, and grief. These themes are alluded to in the psalm, but it goes much deeper. The things I see in it can also set the tone for the entire book of Psalms, in that it there is such a difference between the cursory reading of the psalm and the deeper understanding of it. There are concepts that follow through to the other psalms, and can help understand them with the introduction of Psalm 23.

As noted in the introduction to this book, the translation here is extremely important and fluid. I have modified the translation often, to incorporate the suggestions and ideas others have had. Feel free to compare my translation with whatever you are familiar with. How does it differ?

Remember that all translation is interpretation. If you are lucky enough to work with a partner who happens to know some Hebrew (or if you do), see if you can write your own translation, using the Hebrew to find the deeper meanings in the words, that may lose something in the translation.

All that being said — let's get started!

Psalm 23: Grief

"A Psalm of David"—The first words of the psalm make me wonder: Does this mean David wrote the psalm? Does it mean it was written in his memory? Or for him in his court? The Hebrew word, *mizmor*, is generally translated "a song." So it is a song of David. The key word, for me is "of". If it is of David, and legend has it he wrote all of the psalms, I would then want to know at what point in his life did he write it? Is this a song he would have written in his youth (before or after slaying Goliath); is this a song he would have sung after defeating hordes of Philistines, or when would he have had the wisdom to be able to describe so well what he was up to with this song? The same questions could be asked if it is a song written for him: when would it have been a meaningful song for him to hear? As we look at the psalm, keep these questions in mind–perhaps the answers are actually in the psalm.

"The Holy One is my shepherd..."

Think about what it must be like to be a sheep in a flock. How does a sheep feel about his/her shepherd? I am not kidding: put on a sheep's clothing for a minute and think about what this line is saying. If I am a sheep:

a. I do not get to tell the shepherd what to do.
b. I have no choice about going where the shepherd drives me.
c. I do not get a vote on anything the shepherd does.
d. I am completely dependent on the shepherd, for food, water, and shelter.
e. The shepherd does not solicit or care about my opinions.
f. I do not get to ask the shepherd for anything, and certainly can make no demands of him/her.

These are pretty radical thoughts!

If David, or the author, is saying I am a sheep in the flock, s/he is making precisely these points. If we are in God's flock, we do not get to tell God what to do, where to go, what we need, other than the basics. Our feelings about the shepherd are irrelevant to the shepherd. We are not here to consult, advise, discuss or approve of our shepherd's actions.

So many of us are so disappointed that God does not do what we want. For example:

> Grandma was 109 years old, had two forms of cancer, a broken hip, and extreme dementia. I prayed for her immediate and complete recovery. She died. God was clearly not listening to my prayers. I can't believe in a God that doesn't listen to, or do, what I want.

The example is extreme, but we all know people who made their demands of God, did not get what they wanted, and are therefore no longer going to engage with God—whatever that means. We are supposed to do God's will; God doing our will is magical thinking, not theology. If we are sheep in God's flock we have no choice but to stop kvetching and follow directions.

So why do people get sick and die? Why do accidents or terrible things happen? I believe the answer is: that's the way the world was created. Disease happens, not as punishment, but as natural order of the world. Disasters happen, not because we deserve them in some way, but because the world is imperfect. Our job, as humans, is to work toward the perfection of the world, to make it a better place than it was. In doing so, we are partners in the creative work of God. Doctors, nurses, healing professionals and mental health professionals—we are all doing God's work, bringing greater perfection to the world with our own hands. People die, not as punishment or warning or reward, but because our bodies wear out and things go wrong. We are not perfect.

We don't have to like the reality of being human, but once we begin to accept our own humanity with some humility, we can then deal with hope, within the natural order of the world.

Magical thinking is often the only theology many people have considered. In *Bruce Almighty* (a great flick in terms of theology), God hears everyone's prayers to win the lottery. Everyone wins, which means no one wins. When we engage in magical thinking, we expect God to do what we want. Inevitably, we pray against the natural order of the world. Then we are frustrated or angry because we were unable to influence God's will. The natural order of the world will always win out. If we are sheep in God's flock, we have to accept the natural order of the world: there will be sickness, there will be disasters, and there will be bad things that will happen that we don't want. We have no control over these things, and must surrender to God (the shepherd), that somehow, what we don't want (and what we don't like) is God's (the shepherd's) will. As sheep in the flock, we have no choice but to accept that which we cannot change.

On the other hand, if we as the sheep feel protected and taken care of, we willingly surrender to the shepherd to do the shepherd's job, and we do our job. We stop attempting to order the shepherd around, and we do our best in our own circumstances, within the natural order of the world.

There is also another major issue between the shepherd/sheep; God/humanity. Just as the psalm is talking about two very different species—humanity and sheep, the psalm is speaking in the metaphor of two very different kinds of beings—God and humanity. We are never really going to understand what it is like to be a sheep, and sheep are never going to understand what it is like to be a human. God and humanity have the same problem: we will never understand God. We are very different kinds of beings, as different as sheep are from humans. God may well give us clues into understanding some of what God wants us to understand, but we know as much about God as a sheep knows about a human being.

If we are sheep in God's flock, the question arises: What is the purpose of prayer under these circumstances? If the shepherd is not interested in the feedback from the sheep, is God interested in feedback from us? Is God interested in our prayers? Is prayer intended to influence the shepherd? How does a sheep influence its shepherd? Does it even attempt to do so?

Prayer is reflexive: it is supposed to move us to achieve the goals we want God to do for us. God is available to hear our prayers and to help us find hope. God/the shepherd does not do our bidding but may well be there for us to cry to, and to join us in the surprise and wonder of life that includes the tragedies we wish would not happen. I think God wishes they would not happen to us too. God created the world imperfect so we would have something to do–bring it closer to perfection. The world was created so we could be free thinkers and doers. But God/the Shepherd is not going to do our jobs for us, bail us out when we screw up, or step in when illnesses or tragedies develop that we weren't expecting.

Prayer helps us find a way to have control over our lives and to find the good that is out there. Prayer needs to make sense within the context of being a sheep in God's flock. It doesn't make sense to pray for what is contrary to the natural order of the world. While miracles do happen, we can't depend on them. We can certainly ask, but beyond that, we need to be honest and realistic in our approach to prayer.

You can pray for what's real and what's appropriate as a sheep in the flock: less pain and suffering, increased strength, appetite, courage, and increased ability to share, talk, and connect with the world; for peace and comfort, for less to worry about, or for a release from tension, fear, or anger. You can pray for comfort in the world to come, that loved ones find daily reminders of their relationships and the good times they shared. You can pray for greater awareness of God's/the shepherd's love and support.

You can pray for the serenity to accept the things you cannot change, the courage to change what you can, and the wisdom to know the difference.

Prayer is the bridge between humanity and Heaven, but not a vehicle for making the shepherd do what we want. Prayer focuses more on influencing ourselves to be the best sheep we can be in the flock.

How do we know what God wants us to do? Sheep know what the shepherd wants. God has given us all kinds of helpful hints into what God wants–Torah, Talmud, Midrash, etc.

Being a sheep in God's flock is the theology of many of the psalms: we are different species; we will never understand the Shepherd; we do the best we can to be the best sheep in the flock. We don't get to order God around, and don't get to expect God to do what we want; we do what God wants. Prayer helps us be the best we can be within the natural order of the world— to be partners with God in perfecting the world.

"I will not be overlooked."

This translation/interpretation is radical, but I think makes the most sense of the words. I never understood saying "I lack nothing". Many of us feel we lack; while the psalmist may be speaking in metaphor and not expect us to take "I lack nothing" as literal, it seems to me a misstatement of our situation as humans. How can someone who is mourning the loss of a loved one say they lack nothing? How can someone who is starving say that? How does it work when we as human beings are always feeling like we want more?

> There is a beautiful story about a prince who lived in his father's castle. One day the prince went to his father, the king, and asked to go traveling into the world to discover his fate. He traveled deep into the forest. Soon a huge, moaning giantess who was missing half her

body, limped over a hill. She dragged herself to the water's edge and drank and drank until the lake was dry… She beat the earth with her fists and thundered, "THERE IS NOT ENOUGH!! MY THIRST IS UNQUENCHED!!" The ground shook with her pounding and wailing. Finally, she exhausted herself and slept. When she awoke, she dragged herself back the way she had come.

The prince followed her. She led him to her castle. She lit a fire under an enormous cauldron in front of the drawbridge. She saw a herd of buffalo wander by the castle and she scooped up a dozen of them in her huge hands, tore them limb from limb, and threw them into her cauldron. A flock of geese flew overhead. She reached up and caught a dozen geese, tore them to shreds, and threw them into her cauldron. Then she added a hundred bags of flour, barley, peas, and oats. While the stew cooked, the giantess went in the castle to prepare herself for dinner.

Meanwhile, the prince was hidden in a tree near the cauldron. When the giantess left, he speared a piece of meat for himself and his dog, then hid himself again in the branches of the tree. When the half-giantess returned, she tipped the cauldron to her mouth and swallowed the entire stew. She looked at the bottom of the pot and began to scream, "THERE IS NOT ENOUGH!" She raged, breathed fire, and stomped the ground. After a time of ranting and raving, the half-giantess exhausted herself and, once again, she slept.

As she slept, the prince made a stealthy, speedy retreat. He rode back to his father's castle and right up to the king's throne. The king, amazed at the changes in his son, rushed to embrace him. At his father's touch, the son said, "Father, I have seen life." (King Duncan, *Dynamic Preaching*, 1997, 77.)

Saying I lack nothing, even if it is a hopeful statement, even as it relates to being a sheep in God's flock (where God as shepherd provides everything), leaves me not believing the concept. As a human being, I am always going to want more, and am always going to feel that I lack. It's that basic feeling of wanting more/better/other that drives us forward as people.

The better translation is "I will not be overlooked." It really should be "I will not be missed" (i.e., "the Holy One will count me in"). But since "I will not be missed" could mean its opposite ("no one will miss me") it does not work as the translation. In modern Israel, when a soldier is missing, s/he is *haser(ah)*. The Hebrew in the psalm is the same root, *H-S-R*. This makes sense and is reassuring: The Holy One is my shepherd, and I can count on that shepherd not overlooking me. I am in the flock, and the Holy One counts me in; I have not gone missing. I am right where I should be, in the flock, and in relationship with my shepherd. I count! I matter to the shepherd. This translation makes sense to me, and fits within the imagery—I can rely on the shepherd to make sure I am counted, that I am part of the flock, and that I am a part of the responsibilities of the shepherd. After all the adjusting I have to do, to know that I can't tell the shepherd what to do, it is comforting to know that the shepherd cares enough about me not to leave me behind, not to let me go missing. I may be a sheep in the flock, but I am a sheep that matters to the shepherd!

"God makes me lie down in green pastures;
God leads me beside still waters. God renews my life."

As a sheep in the flock, I expect the shepherd to take care of my basic needs. In this case, as a sheep, I am expecting only the best—green pastures, still waters, and being kept alive. Sheep cannot drink from flowing water (don't ask me how I know that!), but the imagery makes sense. We would expect our shepherd to take us to the best spots, and in so doing, renew our lives and bring us fulfillment.

"God guides me in circles of justice as befits God's name."

This is another radical translation/interpretation. The King James Version (KJV) translates as "paths of righteousness," and JPS translates this as "right paths." But the Hebrew is neither. A *ma'agal* is a "circle," not a path, and *tzedek* is "justice" (though righteousness is not that far off). Yet righteousness feels voluntary, whereas we are commanded to pursue justice. Righteousness also has an implication of self-righteousness; paths of righteousness are for the people who think they are righteous, or who want to be (unless the path itself is righteous, perhaps meaning straight, direct). But it's not an accurate translation at all.

"Circles of justice" leads me in a very different direction. First, circles do not end; paths do. The plural "circles" implies to me that there is more than one, perhaps concentric circles, with different levels of justice for each circle. The pursuit of justice is never ending, always engaging; continuous. Justice is not righteousness; circles of justice lead us to maintaining and increasing justice, not losing track of it.

"Circles of justice" means that justice will happen, even if we don't see it happening. We all know people who do horrible things and seem to get away with them. "Circles of justice" implies that the justice will come to them—they are in the circles of justice.

I have also had students react to circles of justice with thoughts of karma— you get what you put out there. The problem with circles of justice is that we have to trust that they are ongoing, and that the people we know who deserve (and merit) benefits (or punishment) may not experience the justice in front of us. We have to have faith they will get what they deserve.

There is no way out of the circle: we all experience justice for what we do, good or bad, at some point in the circle.

When I was diagnosed with cancer, I never wondered about the circle of justice of it. I lived my life as I lived my life. Illness has nothing to do with justice. God doesn't punish us through illness or reward us through good health. Illness happens as part of the natural order of the world. Parts wear out and go bad. I had many, many years of relatively good health. The question was not "Why me?" but "Why not me?" While living with cancer is not much fun (to say the least), it has been an educational experience for me. Perhaps the circle of justice is enabling me to know first-hand what I have been teaching and talking about, as I have been working with people living with serious illness for my entire professional career. I'd rather not have cancer, all things being equal, but if all things are equal, there's no reason I shouldn't get cancer.

What's the difference between a "circle of justice" and a "right path?" A circle of justice engages me, keeps me working on improving my level of bringing justice into the world. The circle of justice is never-ending. A right path ends; it doesn't lead me back or take me to places of justice at all. It may wall me in, keep me doing right things with blinders on to what is on the sides of the right paths, or tangential to those paths. But the right path ends at some point. Where are we when it does?

Maimonides suggests eight levels of justice in giving. Given this understanding of the psalm, they are concentric circles.

Level 8 — The donor is pained by the act of giving;

Level 7 — The donor gives less than he should but does so cheerfully;

Level 6 — The donor gives after being solicited;

Level 5 — The donor gives without being solicited;

Level 4 — The recipient knows the donor but the donor does not know the recipient;

Level 3 — The donor knows the recipient but the recipient does not know the donor;

Level 2 — Neither the donor nor the recipient knows the other;

Level 1 — The donor gives the recipient the wherewithal to become self-supporting.

As befits God's name: we would expect that either the shepherd or the Holy One would guide us through these circles of justice. Once again, we can't demand anything from the shepherd, but given who the shepherd is, it stands to reason that we would be guided through these circles. It fits with what we can expect from the Holy One.

"Though I walk through the valley of the shadow of death..."

I was in Washington, D.C., at the largest display of the AIDS Memorial Quilt. I went there on behalf of the mothers' group I had formed for mothers who had lost a child of any age to AIDS. It was an activism group, to help them turn their grief into action and to help other mothers going through the nightmare they experienced. They had given me panels to dedicate to the Quilt, and I was on a mission to bring them, to give them into the hands of the Quilt staff.

The Quilt was laid out all along the Mall in the center of the city, going from the Capitol Building to the Lincoln Memorial. The Quilt actually went from near, the Capitol as far as the

Washington Memorial. There were thousands of panels. And on both sides of the Mall were the museums: the Smithsonian, the National Gallery of Art, etc. They were like mountains on each side. As I walked through the panels of the Quilt, read the names and felt the joy in the lives remembered and the horror and grief at their loss, I had a sense that I was walking in the Valley of the Shadow of Death.

Where, what, when, how is this Valley of the Shadow of Death? First, the translation: JPS translates it as a "valley of deepest darkness." Unfortunately, the Hebrew is much clearer: it is shadow (*tzel*) and death (*mavet*). I am not sure why the JPS translation would move away from the word "death," and what is gained by a translation that pretends that it's not death. Is "deepest darkness" a euphemism for death? I guess it doesn't get much darker than death, but why not say it, since it is a translation?

What is the Valley of the Shadow of Death?

Many students have suggested it's when we experience a death, or when we go into a cemetery. But I think all of life, from the moment we are born, is our journey through the Valley of the Shadow of Death. We can all die at any moment, and we live with that knowledge. Life is precious and fragile. We never know when we will die, though we do know that we will die (I hope that's not a surprise for anyone reading this!). Our entire lifetime is life in the Valley of the Shadow of Death!

I used to co-facilitate a Torah study group for people living with serious illness. For some of the participants, this was the only time they left their homes, except for doctors' appointments. It was very holy time. One of the participants, Burt, had prostate cancer. He would say that he knew he would die from the cancer. I would tell him that was nonsense. He could get hit by a bus any day. We never know how we are going to die. And just because he had cancer didn't mean that his life-warranty was worse than mine. I could also get hit by a bus.

A few years after we began working together, Burt had a massive heart attack and died. I spoke at his funeral about how he would have laughed about not dying from the cancer. You just never know.

The struggle is in the Valley of the Shadow of Death that is not a physical place but a time: our lifetime. Every moment we live, we live in the Valley of the Shadow of Death, ignoring most of the time that the shadow is ever-present in our lives. Our journey in the Valley (in life) can be a guided tour, led by the shepherd, or, if we engage our humanity and free choice, it can be a self-guided tour. But we all walk through this valley at all times.

"I will not be afraid of anything..."

This is translated as, "I will fear no evil" in the King James, and JPS says "I will fear no harm." There is agreement on fear. Fear can be paralyzing; it can keep us from moving on in any way. When we are afraid, we are stuck. But in this case, it's fear of "ra," which is "bad." The alliteration in Hebrew is also noteworthy, *lo ira ra*—"I won't be afraid of that which is bad."

This doesn't say bad stuff won't happen. Just that I don't have to be afraid of it. Bad will indeed happen, but being afraid of it means I will be unable to function in the absence of the bad stuff, waiting for it to happen.

King James translates *ra* as "evil." Evil has a connotation which is not present in the Hebrew—it is malevolent or sinful. But that is not what the Hebrew says. There is a huge difference between "evil" and "bad." Translating *ra* as "evil" means that I might not fear sinful behavior, or malevolence, but there is nothing sinful or malevolent in the world of bad things that could happen. Earthquakes, storms, natural disasters are good examples of "bad" that we have no reason to fear, which have no malevolence or sinful behavior attached to them. Translating *ra* as "evil" takes away a lot of the meaning of the word *ra*.

The JPS translation for *ra* is "harm." Once again, the translation misses the mark: bad things can happen that are not necessarily about "harm." I can lose my job because of budget problems where I work. It's a bad thing that can happen, but not about harm. I may not like looking for another job, but there was no intention of harm in laying me off. I may see myself as harmed by the layoff or I may find an even better job. If I do, was there harm? Yes, there would be the emotional and psychological impact of losing a job, but is that a harm I should fear? I can get really sick, and go to the doctor who cures me of the illness. The illness certainly would be defined as *ra*, "bad," but not about harm. Maybe I could even learn something about myself from the illness.

Ra doesn't translate well to English, though. Bad stuff, which I have used in translating *ra*, doesn't sound very sophisticated. I tried malevolence, but that has connotations similar to harm. I found there was really no way to translate it directly. If I am not afraid of "bad stuff," I translate the line as "I will not be afraid of anything." Certainly, I am not going to be afraid of good, so inclusion of good is irrelevant to the translation. Not being afraid of anything is probably the best way to encompass the meaning of *lo ira ra*, but I remain open to suggestions.

"...You are with me..."

The "bad" does not come from God, according to the psalmist, but when it happens, I don't have to fear it. If the psalmist wanted to imply that the "bad" was God's will, he would have. Here again is a point of discussion with people who wonder about the source of bad experiences or events. I don't have to fear anything, good or bad, because God is my shepherd, and if I am walking in the Valley of the Shadow of Death at all times, I have no reason to fear because during the walk in the Valley, God is right there with me. Again, it is not to prevent bad things from happening, since they will, but to provide me with ways to get through that which I perceive as "bad" experiences. If I have God on my side, and I turn to God to carry me through whatever happens, what do I have to fear? I will walk through the Valley of the Shadow of Death confident that I can get through the worst of it, somehow, by turning to God, who will not undo the negative experience, but will enable me to find my way through the experience. I will still have bad things happen, but I will be much better equipped to manage my life through them by an awareness that God is at my side and is rooting for me.

There is a shift here as well, from third to second person: The psalm takes us from the universal to the personal as we journey through the Valley. The first verses refer to God as the Holy One (a direct object). But in this verse it becomes a very personal "You." The entire flock is in the shepherd's care; all people are in God's care as we walk through the Valley. But now, the verse is about a personal relationship, no longer universal. I may be a sheep in the flock, the entirety of which God cares about, but as an individual, God guides me personally. I am not alone as I face the bad things in my life—"You are with me."

"Your rod and Your staff comfort me."

We can reinterpret our pain and reframe our suffering in terms of finding the meanings within the journey. If we can look back at our struggles, hurts, and frustrations (in the light that there was something we gained from the process), we can find meaning and growth within the struggle, from the struggle.

What is a rod and a staff? What's the difference between them? We are back to the shepherd image. The rod is a stick the shepherd uses to prod the sheep along. Or it can be used against wolves and other predators aiming to harm the sheep in the flock. The staff is much longer and has a hook on the end, and the shepherd can lean on the staff. The shepherd uses the staff to pull a sheep back onto the trail if it has wandered off.

They are both implements of discipline, but instead of pain they bring comfort. They are comforting based on the first line of the psalm: "I will not be overlooked." If I go astray, the shepherd will bring me back to safety using implements with which I am familiar, and given my wool coat, neither implement is going to hurt me. I will be brought back to safety, to the flock, and I am comforted by the fact that I will not be lost.

Sometimes we may see our suffering as ways in which the rod and the staff are used to bring us back. But that's not what it's about. God does not use illness and suffering like a rod or a staff—there would be no comfort there. God is compassionate, loving, full of grace and kindness. I could never believe in a God who is so capricious as to use illness, without explanation, as a rod or a staff. How would we know for sure what it was that we did to deserve the illness? What good is a punishment when it doesn't fit a crime?

The rod and the staff are about compassion, loving-kindness, and love. As a sheep in the flock, I have to welcome them since they are part of my protection. There is nothing that can harm me about them; they are implements of love.

"You spread a table before me in full view of my enemies."

This psalm is attributed to King David: at what point in David's life would that attribution apply? Who are the enemies? This is the writing of a man with perspective, looking back at his life. David's enemies are not the Philistines.

Time and again, we see that David is his own worst enemy. The greatest example of that is with Batsheva and Uriah. David has an affair with Batsheva, who is married to Uriah. He ultimately sends Uriah to the front lines in a war, to make sure he is killed so the coast will be clear for his affair with Batsheva, whom he has impregnated. King David committed first degree murder! The entire experience of the Batsheva story demonstrates how David was his own worst enemy.

71

Psalms in the Key of Healing

When the psalms refer to enemies, we can and should see ourselves prominently as our own worst enemy. It's not just David—I have plenty of experience in my life where I can see how I was my own worst enemy. Unfortunately, no matter how aware I am of being my own worst enemy, I never cease to amaze myself at ways in which it is expressed.

It's not just in the things we do. We undermine ourselves with the messages we tell ourselves about what we can and, more importantly, cannot do. We undermine ourselves when we give ourselves negative messages. We undermine ourselves when we believe what others say about us, and by taking other peoples' opinions personally. We undermine ourselves when we are not impeccable with our word. (Ruiz, 1997)

When a table is spread before me in full view of my enemies, it is spread before me—my own worst enemy! But what is on the table? It reminds me of the scene in *Indiana Jones and the Last Crusade.* Indy manages to get to the place where he must make a choice from hundreds of chalices, one of which is the Holy Grail. He has to choose wisely, or he will die. Spoiler Alert: he ultimately chooses the most modest of chalices, which is the correct choice.

The table that is spread before me is just like that array of hundreds of chalices; I have hundreds of choices, hundreds of options. If I choose wisely, great! If I am less wise, I can blame it on my internal enemies, who lead me to make really bad choices. All the options of my life are on the table before me, in the presence of my enemies: me.

So when a table is spread before us in the presence of our enemies, what it really means is: we have choices that appeal to all of our parts and we let our own worst enemies make our choices for us. We have choices; sometimes we choose wisely. Sometimes our enemies win out and our choices lead us to disasters.

"You anoint my head with oil..."

Who is anointed? Kings and priests. Anointing is special. The question here is why would the Holy One anoint me? In addition to placing all those options in front of me, the Holy One is showing me that despite the fact that I am a sheep in the flock, I am important—as important as a king or a priest. My choices matter, and I matter to the Holy One. As an anointed one, I will not be overlooked; I will not be missing.

"...my cup is overflowing..."

We can feel that there is want, and need, or we can see the abundance and make other choices. We can focus on what we lack or focus on what we have. The cup overflowing is a focus not on a half-full glass, or a half empty glass, but rather on a glass that may have some liquid in it, but overflows with the air above liquid, changing the equation completely from what one perceives and can see, to what one believes, and may not be able to see. Overflowing happens.

The Holy One gives me plenty of choices, some of which I may make wisely. My choices matter, as though they were the choices of a king, and I am so blessed! I have so much when I look at it, when I think about it. So much that it overflows everything. There is plenty, if I make wise choices, if I can get my internal enemies to back off enough so that I can see that the Holy One is treating me like a king; is providing for me in abundance. I may not figure out the abundance or precisely what is overflowing from the cup, but it is there nonetheless.

"Only goodness and steadfast love will pursue me all the days of my life..."

Goodness and steadfast love are "running after me," not "following me," as the King James translation indicates. "Following" means they will never catch me—that is not their goal. They are just following, maybe seeing where I am going. It's a terrible translation of the Hebrew, *yirdifuni*, which clearly means "chase after" me. The JPS translation is not much better: "pursue" me. When I am being pursued, it feels sort of passive; not as passive as follow, but not committed to catching me. It is a weak verb. The verb is definitely an active verb in the Hebrew.

Goodness and steadfast love are chasing me. Here's the question: why am I running away from goodness and steadfast love? Another in a long series of unfortunate choices? How can it make any sense that I would run away from goodness and steadfast love? They are out there, available to me, and not only should I let them catch me, I should be running towards them!

Goodness and steadfast love have me in their sights. Perhaps I don't believe I deserve to be caught by them (my internal worst enemies speaking). Perhaps the timing is all wrong: maybe I am too busy with other things to let them catch me.

Whatever the reason, I am being chased by precisely what I would want and running away from it.

"...and I will dwell in the house of the Holy One forever."

When we are caught by goodness and steadfast love, we are dwelling in the house of the Holy One, forever, or as long as we can be in that place where they catch us. Being caught by goodness and steadfast love means getting out of our own way, enabling the experience of the fullness of the cup, the guidance through the Valley of the Shadow of Death. When we are caught by goodness and steadfast love, what happens? We get a taste of what it is like to dwell in the eternity of God's house; we get a taste of the world to come; we get a taste of being in the Presence of the Holy One, even if it's just for a moment.

Moses, our most famous teacher and prophet, asks God to allow him to "behold God's Presence". It's an odd request from a guy who has been sitting on a mountain for 40 days taking dictation from that very God. But God's answer is even stranger: God will allow Moses to see God's Presence, but not God's face—only the back of God—whatever that might be.

Moses is shown that he cannot see God directly. He can only see God's Presence in the past tense, where God has been. So too, with us. We also are allowed to see God in the past tense—where God's Presence has touched us personally and has touched the world. When we are filled with awe and wonder at the world, when we find the places where God has been, we are as close as we can be to God.

In another Biblical "wow" moment, Elijah the prophet told of how he experienced the Presence of God: The Holy One passed by. There was a great and mighty wind, splitting mountains and shattering rock by the power of God; but the Holy One was not in the wind. After the wind—an earthquake; but God was not in the earthquake. After the earthquake, fire; but the Holy One was not in the fire. And after the fire, a thin voice of silence.

God is not in the big deals, the high places, or the "special effects," but rather is present in the voices of silence, touching hearts, shaping souls. According to Rabbi David Wolpe, "God does not reach down to remove tumors. But God grants courage, helps us to hope, strengthens our souls, and stiffens our spine. God helps community cohere. In the stillness and isolation of illness, we can hear God's voice of silence speak to us, and through us." (Wolpe: 1999).

Abraham Joshua Heschel says that all moments are eternal. So when we are caught by goodness and steadfast love, that moment is eternal. We are dwelling in the house of the Holy One forever.

This concept of dwelling in the house of the Holy One forever is probably why the psalm became associated with death. That foreverness seems, on the surface, to be death. But it is much more about getting those incredible moments when we know we are in the Presence of the Holy One, and maybe didn't know it until after the fact. All of us have those moments, when we know that everything is or was different as a result of that incredible moment, whenever it was, whenever it will be. Those moments are permanent, never-ending in their time; eternal.

We should all be working on getting caught by goodness and steadfast love, running away from them as little as possible, and finding those amazing tastes of the eternal.

Pulling It All Together

I am a sheep in God's flock and recognize the difference between our species. I will never understand the shepherd, but I trust that the shepherd will help guide me on my walk through the Valley of the Shadow of Death. Bad things will happen, but I have no reason to fear them, because somehow the shepherd's guidance will help me deal with and overcome the obstacles and bad things I encounter on this journey. I am important to the shepherd, even if I don't understand how that works. I have choices to make and hope that somehow my own worst enemies (me) will not get in the way, and that I will make wise choices from all those incredibly rich options. Goodness and steadfast love want to catch me, and I can stop running away from them. When they catch me I get a taste of what it's like to be in God's Presence forever.

May we all allow ourselves to be caught by goodness and steadfast love, as often as possible!

Psalm 27

Shame and Self Acceptance

Translation and Interpretation by
Rabbi Dr. Rafael Goldstein, BCC

To David

1. God is my light and my help; whom should I fear?
       The Holy One is the strength of my life;
       whom should I dread?
2. When mean-spirited people draw me near to slander me,
       it is these foes and enemies
       who stumble and fall.
3. Should an army surround me, my heart would have no fear.
       Should war come upon me,
       I would still feel secure.
4. Only one thing I ask of God, only this do I seek:
       to dwell in the house of the Holy One
       all the days of my life,
       to gaze upon the beauty of God,
       and to pay attention in God's sanctuary.

5. The Holy One will shelter me in God's *sukkah*;
>> on a bad day the Holy One
>> will hide me in the shelter of God's tent,
>> raise me up safely on a rock.

6. Now is my head high above enemies surrounding me.
>> I sacrifice in God's tent with shouts of joy,
>> singing and chanting a song to God.

7. God, hear my voice when I call;
>> be gracious to me, answer me.

8. To You my heart says: "seek my face."
>> O God, I seek Your face.

9. Do not hide Your face from me;
>> do not turn Your nose from Your servant.
>> You have always been my help so do not forsake me;
>> do not abandon me, my God, my saving power.

10. Even if my father and mother abandoned me,
>> the Holy One would take me in.

11. Teach me Your ways, O God,
>> and guide me on a level path
>> because of my watchful enemies.

12. Do not hand me over to the will of my foes,
>> for false witnesses and unjust accusers
>> have appeared against me, breathing violence.

13. If only I could believe I will yet see
>> the Holy One's goodness while I am alive!

14. Hope in the Holy One,
>> be strong inside, and let your heart be brave.
>> Hope in the Holy One!

לְדָוִד ׀ יְהֹוָה ׀ אוֹרִי וְיִשְׁעִי מִמִּי אִירָא יְהֹוָה מָעוֹז־חַיַּי מִמִּי אֶפְחָד:
בִּקְרֹב עָלַי ׀ מְרֵעִים לֶאֱכֹל אֶת־בְּשָׂרִי צָרַי וְאֹיְבַי לִי הֵמָּה כָשְׁלוּ וְנָפָלוּ:
אִם־תַּחֲנֶה עָלַי ׀ מַחֲנֶה לֹא־יִירָא לִבִּי
אִם־תָּקוּם עָלַי מִלְחָמָה בְּזֹאת אֲנִי בוֹטֵחַ:
אַחַת ׀ שָׁאַלְתִּי מֵאֵת־יְהֹוָה אוֹתָהּ אֲבַקֵּשׁ
שִׁבְתִּי בְּבֵית־יְהֹוָה כָּל־יְמֵי חַיַּי לַחֲזוֹת בְּנֹעַם־יְהֹוָה וּלְבַקֵּר בְּהֵיכָלוֹ:
כִּי יִצְפְּנֵנִי ׀ בְּסֻכֹּה בְּיוֹם רָעָה יַסְתִּרֵנִי בְּסֵתֶר אָהֳלוֹ בְּצוּר יְרוֹמְמֵנִי:
וְעַתָּה יָרוּם רֹאשִׁי עַל אֹיְבַי סְבִיבוֹתַי וְאֶזְבְּחָה בְאָהֳלוֹ זִבְחֵי
תְרוּעָה אָשִׁירָה וַאֲזַמְּרָה לַיהֹוָה:
שְׁמַע־יְהֹוָה קוֹלִי אֶקְרָא וְחָנֵּנִי וַעֲנֵנִי:
לְךָ ׀ אָמַר לִבִּי בַּקְּשׁוּ פָנָי אֶת־פָּנֶיךָ יְהֹוָה אֲבַקֵּשׁ:
אַל־תַּסְתֵּר פָּנֶיךָ ׀ מִמֶּנִּי אַל־תַּט־בְּאַף עַבְדֶּךָ
עֶזְרָתִי הָיִיתָ אַל־תִּטְּשֵׁנִי וְאַל־תַּעַזְבֵנִי אֱלֹהֵי יִשְׁעִי:
כִּי־אָבִי וְאִמִּי עֲזָבוּנִי וַיהֹוָה יַאַסְפֵנִי:
הוֹרֵנִי יְהֹוָה דַּרְכֶּךָ וּנְחֵנִי בְּאֹרַח מִישׁוֹר לְמַעַן שׁוֹרְרָי:
אַל־תִּתְּנֵנִי בְּנֶפֶשׁ צָרָי כִּי קָמוּ־בִי עֵדֵי־שֶׁקֶר וִיפֵחַ חָמָס:
לוּלֵא הֶאֱמַנְתִּי לִרְאוֹת בְּטוּב־יְהֹוָה בְּאֶרֶץ חַיִּים:
קַוֵּה אֶל־יְהֹוָה חֲזַק וְיַאֲמֵץ לִבֶּךָ וְקַוֵּה אֶל־יְהֹוָה:

Psalm 27 has many similar themes that were examined
in Psalm 23, but it goes into further depth when it comes to
dwelling in God's house, and understanding our worst enemies.
It also has an incredible mathematical problem that leads me
to a completely different understanding of the psalm. There
are lots of assurances of God's protection, so many that the
confidence seems even more fragile. The psalm ends with
doubts about God and belief, and with hope that somehow we
will get through that doubt.

"To David..."

Once again, this is a psalm of David. But this time the word
mizmor, "song/psalm," is missing. The introductory statement
is just *l'David.* That leads me to wonder whether it's "to David"

or "of David" or "for David." When other psalms begin *Mizmor l'David*, we translate the *l'* as "of". What difference does it make?

If it's "for" or "to" David, it probably was not written by David. If it's "of" David, we can attribute it to him, even though it is unlikely he wrote it. The missing word, a song, or a prayer, or something to modify the "of David" would be helpful, but the text just says "of David." Once again, if it's of or by David, we have to ask, "at what point in his life could this have been written?" Was he confronting internal demons, guilt, or shame, when he repeatedly assures himself he is not afraid? Was this an affirmation he recited when he was in Saul's court, wreaking havoc under the guise of bringing comfort to the very troubled king? Saul was known to throw spears at him—could that have been the beginning of his response to the fearful things in his life? Or it could be that he was old, facing the death all of us fear, and trying to reassure himself, in the face of the fear of death, that he is with God and has nothing to worry about?

There is a story in the Babylonian Talmud (*Shabbat* 30a-b) that David was anxious about when he would die. So David asked God to let him know when he would die. God replied, "you will die on Shabbat." But God did not say which Shabbat. So David, being the take-control guy that he was, decided that he would study Torah on Shabbat, every Shabbat, every minute of Shabbat, since there was no way the Angel of Death would take him when he was learning Torah. It happened to be the Shabbat of Shavuot when the Angel of Death made the trees rustle outside, distracting David, who got up to go look at what the rustling was about. And so David died.

"God is my light and my help; whom should I fear?...
Should war come upon me, I would still feel secure."

The first few lines are equal to the shepherd imagery in Psalm 23—but God is now seen as a light, help, and strength. With those, there is no need to fear, because God the Shepherd is present. Even when bad people try to slander me (or when

80

challenging parts of myself try to say that I am bad or attest to my failures), these enemies and foes (parts of myself) are doomed, since I know that the good parts will win out. The same is true if "I am surrounded by an army" or at war (self-doubt can feel that formidable); I can be confident because the Holy One is present for me.

This section of the psalm reminds me of the first of Don Miguel Ruiz' Four Agreements, "Be impeccable with your word" (Ruiz, 1997). The psalmist is not being impeccable with his word—especially the words he uses on himself. His internal speaker is saying he is terribly afraid; it is filling him with self-doubt and self-loathing. He sounds so sure of himself, yet twice he says the same "I will not be afraid."

The mean-spirited people who draw the psalmist near are his internal voices. In Psalm 23, we asserted that we are all our own worst enemies. Here is a great example of how that works. "When my inner voices overcome me" or "draw me near to slander me," the slander is all of the terrible things our inner voices tell ourselves. The slander is how we quietly abuse ourselves with self-destructive thoughts. The slander is how we see ourselves as too ugly, too fat, too short, or too stupid (and this is only a short list of some of my own inner voices!). Our inner voices slander us when they say we can't, won't, or don't think so.

> I will not be afraid. According to Harold Kushner, "When the psalmist tells us three times in the first three verses of his psalm that he is not afraid [Psalm 27], the message I hear is that he is afraid, but he is working at mastering his fears. It is like when your young child tells you, 'I'm not afraid of big dogs anymore.' He is really saying that they still frighten him but he is working on his fears rather than giving into them or hiding from them. And where does

81

the psalmist get the courage to stand up against enemies and other dangers? It comes from his faith in God, not a God who protects him from all trouble and danger so that he never has to feel he is facing his problems alone. To the psalmist, God is the source of light, strength and salvation" (Kushner, 2009, 162).

Even if he finds himself completely under siege, surrounded by armies of his enemies, he still is not going to be afraid. Many of us know what it is like to be under siege by our internal enemies: addiction to alcohol, cigarettes, drugs, food, or power can feel like we are completely under attack. We are surrounded by the very things that make us crazy and give us no rest. In the midst of these overwhelming powers, the psalmist says he will have no fear. The first two of the 12 Steps say the same thing:

(1) We admitted we were powerless over alcohol (or drugs) that our lives had become unmanageable.
(2) We came to believe that a Power greater than ourselves could restore us to sanity.

In these verses, the psalmist recognizes that he is powerless in the face of a besieging army, and the only way out for him is through his Higher Power, the Holy One, and therefore, he will not be afraid. It is noteworthy that this echoes the walk through the Valley of the Shadow of Death in Psalm 23:

I will not be afraid of anything
because You are with me.
Only one thing I ask of God, only this do I
seek: to dwell in the house of the Holy One all
the days of my life

to gaze upon the beauty of God,
and to pay attention in God's sanctuary.

This is by far the most difficult and pivotal line of the psalm. The psalmist asks for one thing, but spells out with three very distinct things:

(1) to dwell in God's house all the days of my life
(2) to gaze on the beauty of God
(3) to pay attention in God's sanctuary.

It seems the psalmist was no mathematician: When is 1 equal to 3? These three things are not the same, yet many people try to interpret the three things as though they were one—all part of the same concept of the one thing the psalmist is asking for. But I am unable to gloss over the differences (the three different verbs and the three different nouns).

Where does God dwell? Many people will express two possibilities: (1) Heaven or (2) within each person. The psalmist's theology leads to a personal connection with God, some element of God's dwelling place being both internal and external. So dwelling in God's house "all the days of my life" could mean living with a sense of God as an internal spark and connectedness, or an external connection to that which is beyond us. If we take a both/and approach, dwelling in God's house is dwelling within ourselves, dwelling within the world, and among people who bring awareness of God's external Presence. Dwelling is both in-dwelling, with God inside ourselves or dwelling within the Presence of God outside of ourselves. To dwell in God's house is to live within our own skin and to see how we are reflections of God's image.

To gaze on the beauty of God is not the same as to "dwell." They are different verbs and do not mean the same thing; one cannot say they are equal when they are clearly very different. How do we gaze upon the beauty of God? Based on where God dwells, we can see that beauty is reflected in ourselves or the people around us, and perhaps see that beauty in the natural world (or even the works of our own hands). If we look at dwelling in God's house as dwelling within our own skins, then gazing on the beauty of God would also be reflexive: God's beauty is reflected by us.

> *When God looks in the mirror,*
> *God sees your face.*
> *When you look in the mirror,*
> *you see God's face.*

"To pay attention in God's sanctuary" is a third completely different verb and a third different noun. There is nothing parallel about these lines. The King James version translates *"l'vaker"* as "enquire," and JPS translates it as "frequent." Neither translation is particularly accurate. The Hebrew would commonly be translated as "to visit," but there is an additional meaning of *"l'vaker"* that fits better: "to observe and to have concern for." When you observe and have concern for something, you are paying attention to it.

Bikkur Holim, visiting the sick, is mistranslated. It's not necessarily about simply visiting people who are ill—it's about observing, showing concern, paying attention to them, hearing them. Registering their needs. When we pay attention to people who are ill is when they feel heard. Just visiting anyone can do. Carefully observing and noting their concerns is where the miracles happen when we work with the sick.

Instead of visiting, frequenting, or enquiring, what does it mean "to pay attention" in God's Sanctuary? Again, it's not just visiting, saying "Hi," but having the transformative experience of really paying attention to what happens, and to our experiences within God's Sanctuary. Does coming into that sanctuary in some way transform us? Many of us know that prayer can be hard, especially when said daily. We lose track of the intention of prayer by focusing too much on the form of prayer. Many of us can attend services and be completely unaware of anything meaningful going on, for anyone, especially ourselves. Many of us know how hard it is to really pay attention, not just to the words, the form, but to the intention, the content of the prayers. "*L'vaker b'haychalo*" is to be fully cognizant and fully engaged in the process of transformation which could happen for each of us in God's Sanctuary—to give what transpires our fullest attention and focus. But where is this sanctuary?

Faces

In order to find the solution to this problem, I explored a different issue: the three times God's face (*panim*) appears in this psalm. *Panim* is a place where we come face to face with God. The word comes from the same root word (*pay nun hay*) as "inside" or "inside of the face (*bifnim*)." To stand in front of someone one is *lifnay*—"towards the face." When one takes something in, one brings it *p'nima*—"into the face." The face is the reflection of what is inside, and when Moses sees God's face, Moses looks inside *himself* (Matt, 26). In the Garden of Eden allegory, God breathes life into the first person—the word for breath and the word for spirit are the same word in Hebrew: *neshama*. God breathes our souls into us. There is a duality, of God as external, and God as internal—breathed into us with each breath, dwelling in our very souls.

According to Abraham Joshua Heschel:

> Our faces are reflections of that which is inside us, created in God's image. The intention is not to identify 'the image and likeness' with a particular quality or attribute of man such as reason, speech, power, or skill... It is the whole man and every man who was made in the

> image and likeness of God. It is both body and
> soul, sage and fool, saint and sinner, man in his
> joy and in his grief, in his righteousness and in
> his wickedness. The image is not in man; it is
> man. (Heschel, 1972, 152)

"Let them make Me a sanctuary that I may dwell among them" (Ex. 25:8). Here again the Hebrew may be complicated. In this verse, God says let them make me a *mikdash* (a holy place), and I will dwell *(v'shahanti)* among them. The word is *shahan* has the same root (*shin, haf, nun*) as the Mishkan, the place where God dwells (the Tabernacle, or a building of some kind). *Mikdash/mishkan:* Two words; same concept–a holy place where God resides. If we make ourselves into a sanctuary, we become the place where God resides, internal and external. A *mikdash* can be seen by everyone; perhaps the distinction between that and a *mishkan* is that the dwelling is not visible to everyone.

God's dwelling place is internal, within us. While we see God as both internal and external, the dwelling place is within us; by dwelling in God's house, we dwell within ourselves, fully and completely accepting who we are, inside and outside. This is radical self-acceptance, seeing ourselves as the places where God dwells.

God is a Work in Progress

Another piece of the theology here is that God is a work in progress: Just as God says at the burning bush, "I will be Who I will be (not "I am Who I am," as it is mistranslated)," God is a work in progress; God will not necessarily be the same as God is now. The statement means that God is alive, dynamic, and ever-changing. It does not say God *is*, just as God is now, but rather God will be that which God will be in the future. We are also works in progress, who reflect the God who dwells, in part at least, within each of us, coming into us through our faces. We accept that we, in our reflection of God's image, are reflections of God's beauty. To gaze upon the beauty of God means, in essence, to gaze upon the beauty of ourselves, because God dwells within. The self-acceptance leads us to see the beauty within ourselves, even as we are works in progress—becoming who we will become.

If we are God's dwelling place, then God's sanctuary is us, so checking in with ourselves, being our truest selves, is frequenting God's sanctuary. To dwell in God's house "all the days of my life" means that I seek to find a way to accept myself fully, completely, as I am; to see how I reflect the Presence of God in my life, and how I can serve as God's sanctuary. I am a reflection of God as I am, and as I will be. There is nothing about me that I need to be ashamed of, because all of me reflects God, even those parts of me that I am not all that happy exist. If God did not want me to be me, as I am, and who I am, I would not be here. Every part of me is a reflection of God—even the parts I used to not like.

Shame and Guilt

Shame is defined as when a person feels bad about something intrinsic to themselves; internal (*bifnim:* "inside the face"). One cannot find radical self-acceptance in the face of shame. Radical self-acceptance is about coming to a place of accepting, even of the places where one would have found shame, self-doubt, or self-deprecation.

Shame is a question of one's core, but guilt is about actions one might regret. This psalm highlights the only way to overcome shame—to accept oneself as God accepts you—to dwell fully within the internal and external house of the Holy One.

I can feel guilty all I need to, or all my mother wants me to—but shame? Shame means there's something intrinsically wrong with me, and being created in God's image means that my entirety is a reflection of God, good and challenging. By being one's truest self, one is a reflection of God and has nothing to be ashamed of.

How does shame affect the way we respond to ourselves? How does shame impact helping relationships, like the chaplain-patient relationship? Overcoming shame of ourselves is a major goal of this psalm, leading us to feel accepted, valued, and loved by God exactly as we are. We can certainly work on our behaviors, and the things that we feel guilty about, but we also should rest assured that we have nothing to be ashamed of as reflections of God's image. With someone who is ill, the illness is also part of the reflection of God. All of our parts, all of what makes us who we are, is a reflection of God. Helping people see illness as holy, as a reflection of God's presence, may be difficult to do, but it can lead to real healing and wholeness. Instead of rejecting parts of ourselves, we can see ourselves as entirely reflections of God.

Three Equals One

Three equals one (3=1) when I dwell in my own skin, see the beauty of myself when I am in my own skin, and accept myself for exactly who I am, knowing I am a reflection of God. This is hard for most of us mortals to do, so we hope we can do it often, and pay attention when it happens. Similar to the end of Psalm 23, three equals one when I let goodness and steadfast love catch me; when I can see when we have those moments when our souls open up to experience God dwelling within us and loving us, no matter what.

"The Holy One will shelter me in God's sukkah on a bad day...I sacrifice in God's tent with shouts of joy, singing and chanting a song to God."

You have to wonder about the quality of "God's *sukkah*." Though JPS translates *sukkah* as "pavilion", it doesn't make sense as a translation of *"sukkah"* to me. A *sukkah* is, by definition, a shaky, flimsy, impermanent structure.

When I worked as the Director of Clinical Services for the Center for Spirituality and Health at Mount Sinai Health System in New York City, my office was in the Guggenheim Pavilion. A very sturdy structure, designed by I.M. Pei, replete with glass pyramids on the roof. This pavilion was anything but a sukkah! The Engineering Department built a sukkah each year so we could celebrate the festival of Sukkot. One year, there was a windstorm two days before Sukkot began. It blew over the sukkah, which was, of course, very sturdily designed by the Engineering Department. You'll never find me translating "sukkah" as "pavilion."

A *sukkah* is a harvest booth—a flimsy place where farm workers can go to get out of the sun, to have a little shade. We are told a few things about *sukkot*: they were built when our ancestors wandered in the desert for 40 years, or were built during harvest season after they settled in Canaan. Traditionally, a *sukkah* is made of natural shade-providing elements: the branches of trees and bushes are the portable shade. The problem is: Where would the Israelites get these things during 40 years in the desert? It was not 40 years in a forest! It is much more likely that when they traveled, they carried tents with them, as they are much more portable and accessible. In any case, being sheltered in either God's *sukkah* or God's tent is not much shelter.

There is one other flimsy shelter that we build as Jews, and it offers absolutely no shelter. That is a *huppah*—the wedding canopy. It is the opposite of the *sukkah*, in that it is open on its sides and closed on top. (A *sukkah* has branches through which you have to be able to see the stars, and at least two and a half walls.) The *huppah* has no walls and is all about the top. The *huppah* is supposed to be a symbol of the home the couple is building together. It's open on the sides to show that the home is open for guests and communal support. The only shelter a couple gets under a *huppah* is the shelter they find in each other.

The *sukkah* symbolizes the same idea—the only shelter we really have is not from pavilions or structures, but from the Presence of God with us in the structure. It is traditional to invite special spiritual guests into a *sukkah,* like our ancestors. That is to remind ourselves that God established a special relationship with them and that relationship continues to this day. The shelter we get in a *sukkah* is the shelter of being in the Holy Presence. We reinforce that sentiment when we shake a *lulav* and an *etrog* (palm branch, myrtle, willow and citron) in the *sukkah* in all directions, once again demonstrating that God surrounds us. The *lulav* is also a symbol of body parts—eyes, lips, backbone; the citron—heart. When shaken in the *sukkah* it is a reminder that God is outside us in the *sukkah,* but also within us as symbolized by the body parts. One could see the shaking of the *lulav* in a *sukkah* as bringing the Presence of God into the body, like a lightning rod.

Shaking the *lulav* and *etrog* in a *sukkah* symbolizes perfectly this discussion of where God's dwelling place is: Internal and external.

So what is this sheltering that's in a non-shelter about? The shelter we get from the Holy One is not in the structure. When God shelters me in God's *sukkah*, the only important part is that God provides the shelter. Picture it as being under the wings of the *Shehina*, God's possibly female protective image. (Note the root of the word *Shehina*, is the same root as the word *mishkan*, "dwelling place.")

When the psalmist is placed high on a rock, once again, where is the shelter? If you are high on a rock, there is no physical shelter on any side, except below. It may be a strategically good position in a war, to be able to shoot down at enemies, but it is also a completely vulnerable position: there is no hiding place. So, once again, being placed high on a rock is a restatement of the lack of physical protection—it is God's protection alone that counts. Being in that protection, of course leads to singing, celebration and shouts of joy.

"God, hear my voice when I call; be gracious to me, answer me....

Do not hide your face from me; do not turn your nose from Your servant."

Back to faces! God's face: "Don't hide your face from me, I seek God's face." When we ask God to show God's face to us, we ask to be able to see that Presence within ourselves. When we ask that God not hide God's face from us, we are asking that we be able to understand and feel that Presence of God in even our worst of times, in times when we are fearful, times when our enemies surround us, breathing fire, or when parts of ourselves lead us into really dark places, when we are ashamed of our inner selves.

The psalmist asks God to not hide God's face from him. Again, the issue of faces is an essential part of this psalm—God's face is mentioned three times in it. If we know we cannot see the face of the Holy One, why would God hiding God's face from us be an issue? If you cannot see it anyway, why worry about it?

Here again is the issue of connectedness with God. If God's face is concealed, one cannot connect with God. If one cannot find God's face, one is faced (as it were) with a crisis—there is no connection to God. By asking to remain connected, to not have to go hunting for the connection with God, the psalmist is asking to find and be in the connection, just described, of God being a supportive and reliable protector. Knowing one can have confidence in turning to God (facing God), one can be sure of all of the security described in the previous verses.

This God face led me to understand that the face was a key to understanding the mathematical problem already described. The mention of God's face three times and the three things that are asked for as though they were one, was a clue that understanding the face issues and was a key to an understanding of this psalm.

All of the other translations for the next line, "Do not turn Your nose away from Your servant" translate *af* as "anger"—do not turn away from your servant in anger, and here again we have an interesting Hebrew word. *Af* can mean "anger," or it can mean "nose." Since the psalmist is referring to face so repeatedly in these lines, I can see no reason to translate *af* as anything other than a restatement of "Don't hide your face from me." Translating it to include anger, out of nowhere, doesn't make sense to me. "Turning up one's nose" and "thumbing one's nose" are both common expressions that make sense in this perspective.

Does God have a nose? In terms of imagery, if God has a face, that face would include the features we would associate with a face.

"You have always been my help so do not forsake me; do not abandon me...Even if my father and mother abandoned me, the Holy One would take me in."

While we know that the past cannot predict the future, we rely on our past experience of God as supportive and helpful, and ask for consistency in the future. In prayer, we often remind ourselves of God's saving power, mostly focusing on our ancestors, Abraham, Isaac, and Jacob or the Exodus from Egypt. We rely on these previous experiences to remind ourselves that God has been there for our people previously, and we hope God will continue to "be there" for us, no matter what.

Why and how would a father and mother abandon their child? The clearest abandonment is death. The expectation is that at some point all of our parents will die, and the hope is that they do not outlive their children. (It should be noted, however, that part of the natural order of the world is that sometimes children die before their parents. It's not what we hope for, but it does happen, and unfortunately, more often than we know or want to think.) For many people, the loss of their parents does indeed feel like abandonment. The only relationship for which we are commanded to say Kaddish (memorial prayer) for eleven months is for our parents. For all other relationships, the mourning period is thirty days.

There are other times when parents may be seen as abandoning their children. Sometimes, unfortunately, parents may abandon their children because they don't agree with something they did, or who they have turned into. Sometimes parents express shame regarding their children when they marry people of other religions, cultures, or races. Sometimes, parents have abandoned their children because they are gay, lesbian, bisexual, transgender, etc. If a parent feels shame regarding their child, and they cannot accept them for who they are, this is a direct contradiction to the passages earlier in this psalm saying that we are a reflection of the Holy One, no matter what, and therefore all parts of us, even the parts some parents cannot accept, are loved by the Holy One. The Holy One is not ashamed about any part of us, and expects us, as reflections of God's image, to not be ashamed of ourselves.

Even if my parents abandon me, The Holy One will take me in. This is the image of God as a "super-parent"—the parent above all other parents—who cannot and will not abandon and brings comfort. In the previous line, the psalmist asks God not to abandon, not to forsake, and concludes that God will not do precisely that. In a way, the psalmist has responded to the worry about abandonment—it is not going to happen.

"Teach me Your ways, O God, and guide me... Do not hand me over to the will of my foes..."

The level path reminds us of Psalm 23, the Circles of Justice, which often is mistranslated as "right paths." But here the

Hebrew is clear: it's a straight or level path. It needs to be level, so we don't trip on this path especially because of our watchful enemies. The watchful enemies, again, are parts of ourselves that we know better than to trust, parts that gnaw at us, and give us no rest, our own guilt and our own frustrations. And as self-destructive people, we know how likely it is for us to trip on our journeys. My inner demons, my watchful internal enemies, are always ready, willing, and able to make me trip on any path I set out on.

And my internal demons are ready to pounce at a moment's notice. The failure messages I give myself are more powerful than any external messages from enemies. I am my own false witness when I undermine my own plans, when I repeat lies in my head often enough that I actually believe them, or when I rewrite history to make myself look less responsible for what went wrong. I am my own unjust accuser when I say "I can't" or when I convince myself that I am not "good enough" for whatever task I am trying to get out of.

Moses at the burning bush tries to convince God to choose someone else, offering several reasons:

- When I go to the Israelites and say to them, "The God of your fathers has sent me to you, and they ask me, 'What is the name of this God?'" (In other words, "Who are You?)
- What if they do not believe me and do not listen to me, but say "God did not appear before you?" (In other words, "Why would they believe anything I say? Who am I?")
- Please, God, I have never been a man of words…I am slow of speech and slow of tongue. (In other words, I can't/won't—I am not capable.)

This is a good example of Moses, our greatest leader and teacher being a false witness and unjust accuser against himself.

94

"If only I could believe I will yet see the Holy One's goodness while I am alive!"

I differ from the translations again here. The Hebrew is clear: "If only I could believe." JPS takes the entire meaning out of the statement, by saying, "Had I not the assurance...," and King James says, "I had fainted, unless I had believed." (I have no idea where they got that from.) *Loo-lay* means "if only." The questioning of belief is what this psalm is about. While the psalmist says s/he will not be afraid and will feel sheltered beneath the wings of the Divine Presence in whatever forms that takes (even if s/he is confident that God would never abandon, s/he still has doubts). All people of faith have their doubts.

Mother Teresa wrote:

> Lord, my God, who am I that You should forsake me? The Child of your Love—and now become as the most hated one—the one—You have thrown away as unwanted—unloved. I call, I cling, I want—and there is no One to answer—no One on Whom I can cling—no, no One. Alone ... Where is my Faith—even deep down right in there is nothing, but emptiness & darkness—My God—how painful is this unknown pain—I have no Faith—I dare not utter the words & thoughts that crowd in my heart—& make me suffer untold agony.
>
> So many unanswered questions live within me afraid to uncover them—because of the blasphemy—If there be God—please forgive me—when I try to raise my thoughts to Heaven—there is such convicting emptiness that those very thoughts return like sharp knives & hurt my very soul. I am told God loves me—and yet the reality of darkness & coldness & emptiness is so great that nothing touches

my soul. Did I make a mistake in surrendering
blindly to the Call of the Sacred Heart? *(Come
Be My Light,* 2009)

So many of us can identify with the doubts. The psalmist
is being realistic in recognizing that despite the bravado of the
earlier phrases in the psalm, doubts remain. And this ancient
doubt gives us permission to have our own doubts, to not know
the answers, but to continue as Heschel would say, in awe. There
are many great books for those of us who can't find our way to
believe, or for those who are in a phase of disbelief. It's part of
our human experience to have our doubts at the same time as
we believe.

If only we could believe. If only we could be fully self-
accepting and fully love ourselves! If only we could silence our
internal enemies long enough to fully and calmly see ourselves
as the reflection in God's mirror.

"Hope in the Holy One, be strong inside, and let your heart be brave. Hope in the Holy One!"

The ultimate answer to our doubts is hope. Take the hope inside
and let your heart be brave and strong and hope in God. Even if
we have these crises, when we can't find the way to that radical
self-acceptance, there is still a way: hope. We will come back to
the theme of hope in Psalm 121.

Pulling It All Together

Despite fearfulness, which can be overwhelming, God is on
my side, providing the only real shelter we can get (in knowing
that we are reflections of God, and have nothing whatsoever to
be ashamed of in ourselves). When God looks in the mirror,
God sees my face. God will not abandon me, nor forsake me,
nor be hidden from me. I can find God within my face (inside
me) and outside of my face (outside of me). God's acceptance of

me for who I am and how I am is permanent and unshakeable. Even my illness, disfigurement, physical differences from others reflect God, requiring me to accept myself for who, what, and how I am.

Psalm 71
Confronting Mortality

Translation and Interpretation by Rabbi Dr. Richard F. Address

1. I seek refuge in You, O Lord; may I never be disappointed.
2. As You are beneficent, save me and rescue me.
    Incline Your ear to me and deliver me.
3. Be a sheltering rock for me to which I may always repair;
    decree my deliverance,
    for You are my rock and my fortress.
4. My God, rescue me from the hand of the wicked,
    from the unjust and lawless.
5. For You are my hope, O Lord God, my trust from my youth.
6. While yet unborn, I depended on You;
    in the womb of my mother, You were my support.
    I sing Your praises always.
7. I have become an example for many,
    since You are my mighty refuge
8. My mouth is full of praise to You,
    glorifying You all day long.
9. Do not cast me off in old age;
    when my strength fails, do not forsake me.
10. For my enemies talk against me;
    those who wait for me are of one mind,

Psalms in the Key of Healing

11. Saying "God has forsaken him:
    Chase him and catch him,
    for no one will save him.

12. O God, be not far from me;
    my God, hasten to my aid!

13. Let my accusers perish in frustration;
    let those who seek my ruin
    be clothed in reproach and disgrace.

14. As for me, I will hope always,
    and add to the many praises of You.

15. My mouth tells of Your beneficence,
    of Your deliverance all day long,
    though I know not how to tell it.

16. I come with praise of Your mighty acts, O Lord God.
    I celebrate Your beneficence, Yours alone.

17. You have let me experience it, God, from my youth;
    until now I have proclaimed Your wondrous deeds.

18. And even in hoary old age do not forsake me, God,
    until I proclaim Your strength to the next generation,
    your mighty acts to all who are to come,

19. Your beneficence, high as the heavens, O God,
    You who have done great things;
    O God ,who is Your peer!

20. You who have made me undergo
    many troubles and misfortunes
    will revive me again, and raise me up
    from the depths of the earth.

21. You will grant me much greatness;
    You will turn and comfort me.

22. Then I will acclaim you to the music of the lyre
    for Your faithfulness, O my God;
    I will sing a hymn to You with a harp,
    O Holy One of Israel.

23. My lips shall be jubilant, as I sing a hymn to You;
    my whole being, which You have redeemed.

24. All day long my tongue shall recite Your beneficent acts,
    how those who sought my ruin
    were frustrated and disgraced.

בְּךָ-יְהוָה חָסִיתִי; אַל-אֵבוֹשָׁה לְעוֹלָם.

ב בְּצִדְקָתְךָ, תַּצִּילֵנִי וּתְפַלְּטֵנִי; הַטֵּה-אֵלַי אָזְנְךָ, וְהוֹשִׁיעֵנִי.

הֱיֵה לִי, לְצוּר מָעוֹן לָבוֹא-- תָּמִיד, צִוִּיתָ לְהוֹשִׁיעֵנִי:

כִּי-סַלְעִי וּמְצוּדָתִי אָתָּה.

אֱלֹהַי--פַּלְּטֵנִי, מִיַּד רָשָׁע; מִכַּף מְעַוֵּל וְחוֹמֵץ.

כִּי-אַתָּה תִקְוָתִי; אֲדֹנָי יְהוִה, מִבְטַחִי מִנְּעוּרָי.

עָלֶיךָ, נִסְמַכְתִּי מִבֶּטֶן--מִמְּעֵי אִמִּי, אַתָּה גוֹזִי; בְּךָ תְהִלָּתִי תָמִיד.

כְּמוֹפֵת, הָיִיתִי לְרַבִּים; וְאַתָּה, מַחֲסִי-עֹז.

יִמָּלֵא פִי, תְּהִלָּתֶךָ; כָּל-הַיּוֹם, תִּפְאַרְתֶּךָ.

אַל-תַּשְׁלִיכֵנִי, לְעֵת זִקְנָה; כִּכְלוֹת כֹּחִי, אַל-תַּעַזְבֵנִי.

כִּי-אָמְרוּ אוֹיְבַי לִי; וְשֹׁמְרֵי נַפְשִׁי, נוֹעֲצוּ יַחְדָּו.

לֵאמֹר, אֱלֹהִים עֲזָבוֹ; רִדְפוּ וְתִפְשׂוּהוּ, כִּי-אֵין מַצִּיל.

אֱלֹהִים, אַל-תִּרְחַק מִמֶּנִּי; אֱלֹהַי, לְעֶזְרָתִי חִישָׁה (חוּשָׁה).

יֵבֹשׁוּ יִכְלוּ, שֹׂטְנֵי נַפְשִׁי: יַעֲטוּ חֶרְפָּה, וּכְלִמָּה--מְבַקְשֵׁי, רָעָתִי.

וַאֲנִי, תָּמִיד אֲיַחֵל; וְהוֹסַפְתִּי, עַל-כָּל-תְּהִלָּתֶךָ.

פִּי, יְסַפֵּר צִדְקָתֶךָ--כָּל-הַיּוֹם תְּשׁוּעָתֶךָ: כִּי לֹא יָדַעְתִּי סְפֹרוֹת.

אָבוֹא--בִּגְבֻרוֹת, אֲדֹנָי יְהוִה; אַזְכִּיר צִדְקָתְךָ לְבַדֶּךָ.

אֱלֹהִים, לִמַּדְתַּנִי מִנְּעוּרָי; וְעַד-הֵנָּה, אַגִּיד נִפְלְאוֹתֶיךָ.

וְגַם עַד-זִקְנָה, וְשֵׂיבָה-- אֱלֹהִים אַל-תַּעַזְבֵנִי:

עַד-אַגִּיד זְרוֹעֲךָ לְדוֹר; לְכָל-יָבוֹא, גְּבוּרָתֶךָ.

וְצִדְקָתְךָ אֱלֹהִים, עַד-מָרוֹם:

אֲשֶׁר-עָשִׂיתָ גְדֹלוֹת; אֱלֹהִים, מִי כָמוֹךָ.

תָּשׁוּב תְּחַיֵּנוּ (תְּחַיֵּנִי); וּמִתְּהֹמוֹת הָאָרֶץ, תָּשׁוּב תַּעֲלֵנִי.
תֶּרֶב גְּדֻלָּתִי; וְתִסֹּב תְּנַחֲמֵנִי.
גַּם-אֲנִי, אוֹדְךָ בִכְלִי-נֶבֶל-- אֲמִתְּךָ אֱלֹהָי:
אֲזַמְּרָה לְךָ בְכִנּוֹר-- קְדוֹשׁ, יִשְׂרָאֵל.
תְּרַנֵּנָּה שְׂפָתַי, כִּי אֲזַמְּרָה-לָּךְ; וְנַפְשִׁי, אֲשֶׁר פָּדִיתָ.
גַּם-לְשׁוֹנִי-- כָּל-הַיּוֹם, תֶּהְגֶּה צִדְקָתֶךָ:
כִּי-בֹשׁוּ כִי-חָפְרוּ, מְבַקְשֵׁי רָעָתִי.

Psalm 71

What does it mean to confront one's own mortality? What choices are before each of us as we realize that the bulk of our life has been lived? We do not know, and cannot control, what our future will be. Our time is out of our control in many ways. The passion and power of the High Holy Day prayer *Unetaneh Tokef* ("who shall live and who shall die,") now becomes more real. Is there a rush to do and see more of life, since we do not know how much of that life is still before us? And what of the role of faith? Do some people, as the reality of mortality embraces us, seek a renewed sense of the spiritual that is accompanied by a return to faith, or is that faith renewed in face of the great mystery of death?

Psalm 71 looks at these issues. The classic interpretation of this psalm is that it was written by an elder, looking backwards in many ways, having found security and trust in his faith in God. Looking at an unknown future, the author prays that his faith and God's love will continue to be a strong foundation upon which to live out his life. "He has always had confidence and faith in God in the past, because God was always at this side in time of adversity. So now too. In his old age his faith has not diminished nor wavered" (Rozenberg and Zlotowitz, 1999, 423)

A question for us is, of course: Do we have such faith? As we get older and confront our own life and what comes next, where is our faith? That really is the underlying question in this psalm. One can look at it in a somewhat depressing manner, or one can see in this psalm a person who, secure in their faith, embraces life, knowing that stresses, challenges, and eventually death await us all. Again, the choice is ours.

"I seek refuge in You, O Lord; may I never be disappointed,... for You are my rock and my fortress."

In the opening verse, the author of the psalm speaks of his devotion and faith. God is his Rock, his foundation. God is always with him. This is mindful of a great fear that so many people now speak of as they age. With the blessing of longevity has also come the challenge of increased isolation. How many of us have been with someone who has outlived their spouse, children, or siblings? We are now witnessing a greater number of people aging alone; people with no family to support them. Are they, then, ever really alone? Is God always there to be that spiritual foundation? Is it that rock that provides spiritual shelter? But what if you reject that concept of the present and personal God?

Our psalmist asks for deliverance. From what do we seek deliverance? In our day, we may pray that we are delivered from a life of pain and suffering, an end of life that we face alone. Is there shame involved in losing that quality of life we so prize? Indeed, one of the translations used for "may I never be disappointed *(abushah)*" is as "may I never be put to shame" (ibid). Is this an acknowledgement of a fear we all share that we may spend the last moments, days, months, or years feeling shamed due to incapacity (both physical and mental)? Is this a cry to God to stand with Him and protect Him?

"My God, rescue me from the hand of the wicked, from the unjust and lawless... when my strength fails, do not forsake me."

103

What for us could be the "wicked, unjust and lawless"? For sure there are many trials and challenges as we age. Let us look at these words as symbols, perhaps, of the changes that take place within our world as we get older. Relationships begin to change: our children, if we have them, grow up and leave. We are faced with the challenge of time, of often re-inventing our self. We begin to lose people close to us. Our bodies begin to change, and we become more used to hearing our doctor tell us to remember, "You are not as young as you used to be." We often find ourselves reflecting on our life's journey and recalling that which gave us strength and meaning. Perhaps, in his own way, the psalmist is reminding us that we are on this journey and it may do well to recall that which did give us strength, from the womb to now. He sees that foundation of strength and calls it God. What do you call it?

How have we been an "example for many?" Here is a powerful line to think about as we get older. We meet here the idea of legacy. We ask, "What has my life meant?," or "How shall I be remembered?" This verse speaks to a moment in life when, for some, there is a realization that we will not live forever. Some people repress that feeling; some gradually assimilate that reality and shift from a focus on the material aspects of life to the spiritual. In that transition, there is the rise of the desire to ask what of us do we wish to leave behind? What memory, what gifts of soul and spirit do we wish to be our legacy to children, grandchildren, our community and faith? Have we lived a life that set an example of holiness? As the psalmist reflects, he seems secure in the knowledge that he has, and the reason for that is that he has had God as his refuge from before his birth. That security of faith has allowed him to set that example of a life of holiness. It is as if he is channeling all of Leviticus 19 and the instructions on how to live a holy life. Why do we honor parents? Why do we observe our rituals? Why do we deal honestly in the marketplace? Why do we treat each other as we would like to be treated? Because *ani Adonai*—I am God—says

Torah. Likewise, our author is secure in the fact that his faith and his God has surrounded him and provided him with a path of righteousness. And what of us?

Yet even the psalmist knows that changes may be taking place. The concepts and fears of the wicked and unjust are present as we age. The dismal vision of part of Ecclesiastes 12:1-7 haunts so many, so our psalmist cries out in the privacy of his soul, asking that, as he ages, he is not cast aside. How relevant is this one verse for so much of what we are experiencing today. The recent pandemic threw back the curtain to a harsh reality in care homes and hospitals, of too many elders literally being forsaken. Again, the fear of being alone and abandoned was reported regularly and gave rise to articles and conversations on a new type of ageism. One of our societal challenges now emerging is this resurgence of ageism. In her book *Elderhood*, Louise Aronson speaks to this rise and what she observes as:

> the widespread need to hold older adults apart...
> We treat old age as a disease or problem, rather
> than as one of the three major life stages. We
> approach old age as a singular, unsavory entity
> and fail to adequately acknowledge its great
> pleasures or unique attributes, contributions,
> physiology, and priorities of older adults.
> (Aronson, 2019, 70-71)

"Do not cast me off" says the psalmist, and one can wonder if that also, in a very symbolic way, is a cry from each of us as we face mortality: "Do not forget me." Is he saying that while people and generations may forget who we were, God will never forsake us? It is sometimes said that we will be remembered as long as there remains someone to say Kaddish for us. The author of Psalm 71 has no worry, for he has faith that God will always be with him.

"For my enemies talk against me; those who wait for me are of one mind ...let those who seek my ruin be clothed in reproach and disgrace."

One can indeed take these words literally: here is a man who may have had enemies. We know that these types of people will go after the righteous and try to diminish one's faith. We also know that a person's own faith can be challenged by life events—events over which he often had not control. Is this enemy then doubt? Is this enemy that we see in these verses the events in life that spread fear and doubt within a person of faith. Is this enemy that we read about the "why is this happening to me?" question that we all meet in our life's journey? Is that what is chasing this psalmist? Are these fears that need to be defeated, perished? Do these verses trigger in us the doubts we may have about our own future, about the mystery of death and the possible choices that we may have to make?

As for me, I will hope always, and add to the many praises of You.

"My mouth tells of your beneficence of your deliverance all day long though I know not how to tell it...O God, You who have done great things; O God, who is Your peer!"

Yet, the psalmist is sustained by hope. A very Jewish ideal, is it not? He is accepting, it seems, the reality of his age and the fact that he may not have many years left. He has lived a righteous life and instead of retreating in fear, he hopes. He praises God again, his source of strength from his youth. In these verses, the writer, in his experiencing the wondrous deeds of God, reminds us of the value of *hakarat hatov*—"gratitude." He is grateful for the blessings he has been granted and for the faith that has sustained him.

We see again a very meaningful ideal of Jewish life in his wish to continue to express his faith and to tell of God's deeds even to the next generation. How important is this for us today? Here is a glimpse into something that we so often forget personally and communally. It is a fact that we are part of an on-going chain of tradition and peoplehood. What are we but representations of spiritual transition? By how we live (that example again) we transmit values and beliefs from generation to generation (*l'dor vador.*) The acceptance of this role can be life changing. We are not isolated in the vast universe. Rather, we are vehicles that link generations through deeds; what we do and how we choose to act is transmitted to "all who are to come."

"You who have made me undergo many troubles ... how those who sought my ruin were frustrated and disgraced."

Again, we see the unbridled faith in the author of Psalm 71. He has a classic theology in that he sees that even his "troubles and misfortunes" are a result of God's actions. Yet he has faith —faith that even if there are to be more of these as he ages, his faith in God will prevail. God will raise his soul and spirit from the depths of despair, and he will continue to sing God's praises, even to the end of life. What a gift this author has! He is so much more secure in his beliefs than so many moderns. God is in control; God has been with him from the womb. Even though he may fear aging, he prays that he is not cast off in that age, and knows that, as he has led a life of example, God will sustain him, even in moments of despair.

How many of us can model this psalm? How many of us believe in these ideals? How many of us, as we reflect on our life, can say that we stand with the psalmist, bathed in the glow of absolute faith, a faith that sustains us even as we may fear our own end?

Psalm 90
Music

Translation and Interpretation by
Rabbi Dr. Shira Stern, BCC

1. A prayer of Moses, God's messenger
   O God, You have been our refuge in every generation.
2. Before the mountains came into being,
   before You brought forth the earth and the world,
   from the beginning of the world to the end,
   You are God.
3. You return us to [a state] as though we were dust;
   You decree: "Return, you mortals!"
4. For in Your sight a thousand years
   are as yesterday once it is gone,
   as a watch in the night
5. You envelop us in a dream-sleep which is fleeting;
   we are like grass that renews itself:
6. at daybreak it blooms;
   at dusk it withers and dries up.
7. [Like the grass], we are consumed by Your anger; and
   we are petrified by Your searing fury.
8. You have laid out our sins before You,
   [Even] the errors we made during our youth.
9. All the days we [wasted] were gone because of Your anger,

We ate up our years like a thought [that vanishes.]

10. The span of our life is 70 years,

   or, given strength, 80 years;

   but the best of those years

   are plagued with troubles and pain [heaviness].

   They pass by quickly, and they disappear.

11. Who can know the true impact of Your anger?

   Your fury is in concert with the fear we have of You.

12. Teach us, therefore, to number our days

   that we will bring a heart of wisdom.

13. Turn away [from Your anger,] God, and return to us

   How long must we wait for Your mercy?

14. Fill us up in the morning with Your loving-kindness,

   so we will sing out and be joyful all our days.

15. Cause us to rejoice in direct proportion to the days

   that you have brought us pain,

   the years when we experienced

   all that afflicted us [evil].

16. Let Your people witness Your loving deeds,

   Your glory be seen by their children.

17. May Your favor, O God, be upon us.

   May the work of our hands flourish;

   O, may the work of our hands endure!

תְּפִלָּה לְמֹשֶׁה אִישׁ־הָאֱלֹהִים אֲדֹנָי מָעוֹן אַתָּה הָיִיתָ לָּנוּ בְּדֹר וָדֹר:
בְּטֶרֶם | הָרִים יֻלָּדוּ וַתְּחוֹלֵל אֶרֶץ וְתֵבֵל וּמֵעוֹלָם עַד־עוֹלָם אַתָּה אֵל:
תָּשֵׁב אֱנוֹשׁ עַד־דַּכָּא וַתֹּאמֶר שׁוּבוּ בְנֵי־אָדָם:
כִּי אֶלֶף שָׁנִים בְּעֵינֶיךָ כְּיוֹם אֶתְמוֹל כִּי יַעֲבֹר וְאַשְׁמוּרָה בַלָּיְלָה:
זְרַמְתָּם שֵׁנָה יִהְיוּ בַּבֹּקֶר כֶּחָצִיר יַחֲלֹף:
בַּבֹּקֶר יָצִיץ וְחָלָף לָעֶרֶב יְמוֹלֵל וְיָבֵשׁ:
כִּי־כָלִינוּ בְאַפֶּךָ וּבַחֲמָתְךָ נִבְהָלְנוּ:
שת [שַׁתָּה] עֲוֺנֹתֵינוּ לְנֶגְדֶּךָ עֲלֻמֵנוּ לִמְאוֹר פָּנֶיךָ:
כִּי כָל־יָמֵינוּ פָּנוּ בְעֶבְרָתֶךָ כִּלִּינוּ שָׁנֵינוּ כְמוֹ־הֶגֶה:
יְמֵי־שְׁנוֹתֵינוּ בָהֶם שִׁבְעִים שָׁנָה
וְאִם בִּגְבוּרֹת | שְׁמוֹנִים שָׁנָה וְרָהְבָּם עָמָל וָאָוֶן כִּי־גָז חִישׁ וַנָּעֻפָה:
מִי־יוֹדֵעַ עֹז אַפֶּךָ וּכְיִרְאָתְךָ עֶבְרָתֶךָ:
לִמְנוֹת יָמֵינוּ כֵּן הוֹדַע וְנָבִא לְבַב חָכְמָה:
שׁוּבָה יְהוָה עַד־מָתָי וְהִנָּחֵם עַל־עֲבָדֶיךָ:
שַׂבְּעֵנוּ בַבֹּקֶר חַסְדֶּךָ וּנְרַנְּנָה וְנִשְׂמְחָה בְּכָל־יָמֵינוּ:
שַׂמְּחֵנוּ כִּימוֹת עִנִּיתָנוּ שְׁנוֹת רָאִינוּ רָעָה:
יֵרָאֶה אֶל־עֲבָדֶיךָ פָעֳלֶךָ וַהֲדָרְךָ עַל־בְּנֵיהֶם:
וִיהִי | נֹעַם אֲדֹנָי אֱלֹהֵינוּ עָלֵינוּ
וּמַעֲשֵׂה יָדֵינוּ כּוֹנְנָה עָלֵינוּ וּמַעֲשֵׂה יָדֵינוּ כּוֹנְנֵהוּ:

For forty years, I have been drawn to Psalm 90: it is so rich with emotional angst, hope, fervent prayer, and insight. It speaks of sin and forgiveness, wrong-doing, and redemption. I have read it and reread it, but never in its entirety. While it is well known for establishing the lifetime of human beings as "three score and ten or with strength, four score…" and also known for pointing out that God requires we acknowledge our sins and that we repent ("Return, you mortals!"), I always continue until I reach verse 12: "Teach us to number our days, that we may grow a heart of wisdom." It was *the* verse that carried me through those days when I had to remind myself that I had to make every day count, to not waste opportunities that I would

111

later regret. It was *the* verse that helped me look back on a day, or a week, or a year, to take an accounting of what I had done, to pay attention to the details of everyday life that might have been forgotten or ignored along the way. It was *the* verse that reinforced for me how important it was to make meaning (and make meaningful), each encounter with another human being.

When I thought of Psalm 90, I realized that every sermon I had ever written had verse 12 embedded in its message.

Now, I studied this piece anew, and decided to continue to the end of the psalm. And my heart began to sing—suddenly, I was transported back to a time when joy and sadness, fear and relief, anxiety and gratitude shaped so much of my chaplaincy.

When I first became a chaplain at Memorial Sloan-Kettering Cancer Center in New York City, I was assigned to the Pediatrics Unit and the Breast Cancer floor. As a young woman, walking among other women who were contemplating radical mastectomies was daunting for me. Often, I couldn't find the words to soothe or comfort my patients. The halls were quiet, sometimes interrupted by a disembodied TV voice or a sob after a doctor left a room.

I thought I should distract them, but found that my silence was the only tool in my pastoral care kit; in my quiet, these women found their voices. They talked about their feelings about their femininity; they were sure their husbands would leave them; they were hopeful that surgery and chemo would eradicate the cancerous cells, but they knew the cancer could return.

In Pediatrics, the atmosphere was completely different. The rooms were bright, the decorations large and lovely, and the playroom was the focus of every child who felt well enough to get out of bed. On that floor, there was noise: a great deal of laughter and squeals and quiet, contented talk. It took me a while to get used to that, because that floor should have been the most tragic place in the universe. How could these kids work at their puzzles, play board games, and throw Nerf balls while the specter of cancer loomed over them? For many clergy, CPE students, and seminarians, those questions were overwhelming; few of us who volunteered at the hospital were willing to be assigned to it. For me, even in the fear and pain, there was so much hope.

I remember teaching the *Four Questions* for the Passover *seder* to an eight-year old with leukemia; playing the tambourine with the music person who came to offer her gifts; singing Simon and Garfunkel melodies to teens as they waited for their chemo drip to empty. But I never used those skills I developed with adults; I assumed—incorrectly—that when grown-ups were struck with illness, they didn't want to be reminded of the harmonies from the world outside; they were living in their heads.

It took me to my third unit of Clinical Pastoral Education, and a wiser colleague than I, to realize what I was missing. I am indebted to Rabbi Stephanie Dickstein, for her inservice lesson. I would sing at funerals; I would sing on my way home from work or school; I would sing in the classroom. But somehow, in the intimacy of a hospital room, it never occurred to me how powerful a tool I was leaving at the door.

And so I began to sing. To everyone.

Sometimes I sang the ritual of welcoming the Sabbath for a patient unable to say the prayers himself, because he was ventilated; often it was a series of healing melodies that would carry me through the long hours beside an extubated person waiting to die. And sometimes it was a lifeline I would offer to a Red Cross client I had met while deployed as a volunteer Disaster Spiritual Care chaplain.

In my nearly two decades working for the Red Cross, I learned from those we served, from those with whom I worked side-by-side, from the leaders who would share their wisdom before we set out in the morning, to frame our day. When it was my turn to inspire, I shared with my fellow Red Crossers stories of the people whom we had helped, or how a blessing seemed to bring a sense of peace to those we met.

Each morning I would wake up thinking, "What could I use today from my pastoral care tool box that would be appropriate and welcomed by survivors?" What words of wisdom could make any of this better, given the enormity of their loss in the hurricanes, the fires, the bombings?

Listening to those stories that touched my heart, that moved me in ways I cannot articulate, reinforced for me how important it was to listen to *their* narrative so that I could respond appropriately. Sometimes, I was silent, but if I offered to sing a blessing, the answer was always "yes."

One encounter in particular I will always carry in my heart: In a small rural town in West Virginia, my team was visiting an elderly woman who had been devastated by a flood they called "The Once in a Century." While my colleague filled out forms with the adult son and processed the Red Cross card to defray funeral expenses for their loved one, I knelt by his mother, who sat quietly in rocking chair, with a handmade quilt on her lap and a blanket on her shoulders, despite the 85-degree heat. "How do I do this," Betty asked. "How do I go forward without him? We were married for 68 years, and I was ten when we met in elementary school."

"Tell me about Bill," I said. And then I waited. Eventually, she painted me a wonderful life review, which only underscored how much this couple loved each other. She told me:

> Bill built this house with his own hands, and we were happy here, which is why I never put him in a home after he developed dementia. I took good care of him. I was the only one who could take care of him as he deserved. So when the waters started to rise, and I couldn't get us out the door, I walked and walked and walked him around the living room so he wouldn't drown. I did that till I could do no more, and

then we sat down on the couch and he put his head on my shoulders. Every 10 minutes, I'd say, "Now look at me and smile, Bill,'" and he would. Until one time, he didn't pick up his head at all. Shortly after, those nice firemen broke through my living-room picture window and rescued us in a rowboat. But my love was gone. He was there, and then he wasn't. He had died because of the cold water. I can't seem to warm up anymore. I've been living in blankets for days. I can't seem to shake this off.

I watched her rocking as she spoke, holding my hands in hers. And I offered her a song:

> Oh Guide my steps,
> and help me find my way,
> I need Your shelter now,
> Rock me in Your arms
> and guide my steps,
> and help me make this day,
> a song of praise to You,
> Rock me in Your arms
> and guide my steps.
> *Ufros aleinu, sukkat shlomeha*[1]

I translated the Hebrew as "enfold me (us) under Your shelter of peace …" I went to the wake, and the funeral, and each time I saw her—she would kiss my hands and ask me to sing her *her* blessing.

Betty taught me the healing power of the human voice, raised in song: it can soothe us; it can calm us down, even when it comes from a stranger, even when some of the words are unusual.

---

1. English words by Debbie Winston and Hebrew text from the Sabbath liturgy.

Psalms in the Key of Healing

Familiar music can transport us to another time in our lives when we were with the ones we loved who have since left this world. Psalm 23 and Psalm 121 are most often associated with funerals, when the slow melodies accompany our sobs. But music can also bring us back to a place where we were happy, like hearing the strains of a lullaby. A song on the radio can bring us to the first dance at our wedding. Or the sound of a high school band at the football game can return us to when our children were… children still.

Music has healing powers and the human voice heightens that power. For several years I was the community chaplain in suburbia, and my job entailed visiting assisted-living and long-term care facilities, as well as acute-care hospitals. Once a month, at one nursing home in particular, I would visit late enough on Friday so that one could legitimately usher in the Sabbath. Nurses' aides would assemble 25-30 residents in a large room, gather them around a makeshift ritual table, set out the grape juice in tiny medicine cups, cut *hallah* bread in small, manageable pieces, and leave me alone with the residents.

A few people actually looked forward to this monthly event, but most residents would sit quietly in a semi-sleep, unresponsive and mute—until I began to sing familiar melodies. Suddenly they would come alive, eyes wide open, heads up, and we would raise the rafters. If I struggled with some words or verses, they would fill them in without hesitation. They belted out the songs they remembered from childhood and would teach me special versions of songs in Yiddish that I had never heard. And when I was inspired to learn a song of my own to share with them, they cried, held my hands and kissed them. When the final refrains were done, they retreated back into their shells, though with a little more color in their cheeks, and a vigor that had not been there before. For me, it was proof that music touches a different part of the brain and heart, and I used it to full advantage.

As chaplains we can harness whatever healing modalities we have—if you have a good voice: sing. If you don't, download songs to play to patients. Ask them what they love to hear, and give them that musical interlude, that respite from the mechanical beeps of a hospital room, to help in the healing process.

We humans sing to show joy, articulate sorrow, and show our longing and gratitude to God. Singing is part of our textual and experiential memory. At the most dramatic times, even our biblical ancestors used music to describe significant moments. Moses sang the Song of the Sea: "I will sing to *Adonai*, for God is highly exalted: horse and rider God threw in the sea" (Exodus 15:1). Miriam picked up her timbrel, gathered everyone together and sang: Sing to *Adonai*, for God is exalted! Horse and rider God has thrown in the sea" (Exodus 15:21).

In fact, the Bible attributes three entire songs to Moses: the Song at the Sea (in Exodus 15), the final poem at the end of Deuteronomy (32:1-52) and this very psalm, Psalm 90, which is attributed to Moses due to word similarities and construction. There are nearly a hundred instances of Israelites singing, the majority of which can be found in Psalms, most of which were attributed to King David. King David used his harp to heal King Saul: "David took a harp and played with his hand: and Saul was refreshed, and was well, and the evil spirit departed from him" (1 Samuel 16:23).

In his book, *Music Physician for Times to Come*, Don G. Campbell reminds us that, "[m]usic has always been considered a bridge to God. From the earliest chants of religious systems in both East and West, the sacred power of word and voice has been recognized as the communion between humans and the Divine."(Campbell, 1991, 330)

Music is good medicine. Just as Norman Cousins discovered alternative therapies to help him overcome a seriously debilitating, near fatal disease, studies indicate that music can increase our level of endorphins. In Don Campbell's *The Mozart Effect*, "the healing chemical; created by the joy emotional richness in music ... enable the body to create its own anesthetic and enhance the immune system."(Campell, 2001, 71). Furthermore, there are a growing number of healthcare institutions around the world which find significant benefits from music for patients and staff. Those surgeons who listened to the music of their choice while operating were found to have lower blood pressure and a slower heart rate and could perform mental tasks more quickly and accurately. Patients exposed to fifteen minutes of soothing music required only half the recommended doses of sedatives and anesthetic drugs for painful operations. And harp music has been prescribed instead of tranquilizers and painkillers for cancer patients (ibid., 132-33).

Chemotherapy and dialysis patients use music to ease through the procedures; people undergoing root canals and MRIs turn up the headphones to compensate for the grating, violent machinery noises, and New Yorkers listen to music as protection when they ride the subway. In each instance, music —often something one can sing along with—becomes the balm that promotes well-being. "Without a doubt," states Raymond Bahr, M.D., Director of Coronary Care at St. Agnes Hospital in Baltimore, Maryland, "Music therapy ranks high on the list of modern-day management of critical care patients...Its relaxing properties enable patients to get well faster by allowing them to accept their condition and treatment without excessive anxiety." (Gaynor, 2004, 133).

So I return to my text.

"Fill us up in the morning with Your loving-kindness, and we will sing out and be joyful for all the rest of our days"

Rashi, the 11th-century rabbinic commentator writes about this verse: "On the day of the redemption and the salvation, which is the morning of the night of trouble, the sighing, and the darkness..." I once sat for hours with a patient who was scared to fall asleep, lest she not wake up. So I held her hand, saying nothing, humming softly till her eyes closed and her breathing became regular. Each time I stopped, she stirred; she sighed. And the darkness enveloped me as well as her. I don't know who was more surprised when at dawn, she woke to find me still sitting in that chair, still humming.

For me, music—with and without words—is prayer, and because it doesn't *require* a response from the listener, it is almost universally welcomed. Whether it is hearing a choir or Yo-Yo Ma playing Bach's *Six Unaccompanied Cello Suites* in one sitting, listening to music brings me closer to God. And for many, it can be a saving grace. *"God is my strength and my song, and God has become my salvation"* (Psalm 118:14).

"Cause us to rejoice in direct proportion to the days that you have brought us pain, the years when we experienced all that afflicted us [evil]."

I have listened to so many patients mourn the time they have lost being ill—time with their families, their friends, their work, and themselves. So often I have wished that those precious moments could be restored to them as compensation for the long hospital stays, the excruciating remedies, the unrelenting pain.

Sometimes, the opposite is true: life is full of promise one day and bleak the next. My very first patient at Memorial was a 65-year-old woman named Sarah. She told me how diligently she had worked along with her husband, even when her children were young: they had shortened or missed vacations or days off, because they knew that when they retired, they would have all the time in the world to enjoy themselves. During her exit health exam, the doctor discovered stage 4 breast cancer which had by then metastasized to her liver. She was given three months to live.

All of a sudden, I find myself returning to my favorite verse verse 12: *"limnot yameinu ken hoda (*Teach us to number our

119

days) " "*v'navi levav* **hohmah** (that we may attain wisdom). The Hebrew word *navi* can mean "prophet" if it is translated as a noun. But Rashi points out that it must be translated as a verb: "to bring," so that the verse is read: "...that we will *bring* a heart of wisdom."

That is a clarion call for all chaplains, all clergy, and all students of the mind/body/soul. It is our task to bring those we serve to hearts of wisdom. To do so, we must begin with ourselves. I needed to learn how my voice could open the hearts of others, offer them comfort, insight or the ability to survive the next hurdle, the next test, the next crisis. I needed to know that when I sang, at times I would have to show my vulnerability, as when my voice would break with emotion. I needed to accept that that was all right.

I am learning to master the ability to cry—either with joy or with sorrow—and sing at the same time because I now know that the music has the power to transcend the mundane; to bring in the holy.

Teach us, God, to number our days, so that we will bring a heart of wisdom. Fill us up in the morning with Your loving-kindness, so we will sing out and be joyful all our days.

Psalm 92

Growing Older
Translation and Interpretation by
Rabbi Dayle A. Friedman, BCC

1. A sacred song for the day of rest.

2. When I am aware of my blessings, I praise You.

3. I arise each day grateful for Your love,
     and I retire enfolded in Your constant presence.

4. I make a joyful noise. I rejoice in Your creation;

5. I sing of Your handiwork.

6. I marvel at Your great deeds,
     yet so much is hidden from my understanding.

7. Anyone with sense recognizes:

8. Malevolence flowers like grass, and cruelty abounds,
     but they will not endure.

9. But You, Exalted One, are Eternal.

10. Malice and injustice will ultimately disintegrate
     and disappear.

11. You empower me; You refresh me.

12. I see myself beset, yet I hear this promise:

13. If we live with integrity, we shall flourish like the palm tree,
     casting shade like the cedars of Lebanon.

Psalms in the Key of Healing

14. Plant us in the house of the Eternal;
    let us flower in the presence of our God.
15. Let us bear fruit in old age; juicy and fresh we'll remain.
16. We will affirm: God is my Rock, unfailing and unflawed.

מִזְמוֹר שִׁיר לְיוֹם הַשַּׁבָּת:
טוֹב לְהֹדוֹת לַיהוָה וּלְזַמֵּר לְשִׁמְךָ עֶלְיוֹן:
לְהַגִּיד בַּבֹּקֶר חַסְדֶּךָ וֶאֱמוּנָתְךָ בַּלֵּילוֹת:
עֲלֵי־עָשׂוֹר וַעֲלֵי־נָבֶל עֲלֵי הִגָּיוֹן בְּכִנּוֹר:
כִּי שִׂמַּחְתַּנִי יְהוָה בְּפָעֳלֶךָ בְּמַעֲשֵׂי יָדֶיךָ אֲרַנֵּן:
מַה־גָּדְלוּ מַעֲשֶׂיךָ יְהוָה מְאֹד עָמְקוּ מַחְשְׁבֹתֶיךָ:
אִישׁ־בַּעַר לֹא יֵדָע וּכְסִיל לֹא־יָבִין אֶת־זֹאת:
בִּפְרֹחַ רְשָׁעִים | כְּמוֹ עֵשֶׂב
וַיָּצִיצוּ כָּל־פֹּעֲלֵי אָוֶן לְהִשָּׁמְדָם עֲדֵי־עַד:
וְאַתָּה מָרוֹם לְעֹלָם יְהוָה:
כִּי הִנֵּה אֹיְבֶיךָ | יְהוָה
כִּי־הִנֵּה אֹיְבֶיךָ יֹאבֵדוּ יִתְפָּרְדוּ כָּל־פֹּעֲלֵי אָוֶן:
וַתָּרֶם כִּרְאֵים קַרְנִי בַּלֹּתִי בְּשֶׁמֶן רַעֲנָן:
וַתַּבֵּט עֵינִי בְּשׁוּרָי בַּקָּמִים עָלַי מְרֵעִים תִּשְׁמַעְנָה אָזְנָי:
צַדִּיק כַּתָּמָר יִפְרָח כְּאֶרֶז בַּלְּבָנוֹן יִשְׂגֶּה:
שְׁתוּלִים בְּבֵית יְהוָה בְּחַצְרוֹת אֱלֹהֵינוּ יַפְרִיחוּ:
עוֹד יְנוּבוּן בְּשֵׂיבָה דְּשֵׁנִים וְרַעֲנַנִּים יִהְיוּ:
לְהַגִּיד כִּי־יָשָׁר יְהוָה צוּרִי וְלֹא־עלתה [עַוְלָתָה] בּוֹ:

Psalm 92 is the only one of 150 *tehillim* that is dedicated to the Sabbath, Shabbat. Shabbat is the last day of the week, a day of rest and renewal. This day can be seen as parallel to aging—the last phase of the life cycle. The psalm expresses widely disparate moods and images—delight, satisfaction, despair, and hope. We will endeavor to see what we might learn about the journey of growing older from the psalmist's words.

122

Gratitude

The first section of the psalm expresses gratitude:

> When I am aware of my blessings, I praise You.
> I arise each day grateful for Your love,
> and I retire enfolded in Your constant presence.
> I make a joyful noise. I rejoice in Your creation;
> I sing of Your handiwork.
> I marvel at Your great deeds,
> yet so much is hidden from my understanding.

As we grow older, we may become especially aware of our blessings. For some elders, this awareness is present in the very moment they inhabit.

Rabbi Schwartz was 95 when I encountered him in the hospital. He had been a towering figure, not only in his synagogue, but in the larger Jewish community. Now, he was recovering from yet another bout of congestive heart failure. He was hooked up to a feeding tube, an IV pole, and a heart monitor. He looked shrunken as he lay in the bed. He was gazing at the window when I entered his room. I asked, "What are you thinking about as you lie there, Rabbi?" In my arrogance, I thought I knew what he would say: some variant of *ad matai* (how long, O God?). What he actually said was, "I'm thinking of how glad I am to be alive. Look how beautiful the trees are outside my window!"

Rabbi Schwartz placed his gaze on beauty, rather than on his obvious discomfort and pain. An elder's awareness of mortality heightens appreciation for magical moments, loving relationships, and pleasure. A 95-year-old woman reveling in celebrating Hanukah with her family might find the moment charged with particularly intense and poignant pleasure as she wonders, "How many more times will I get to see the lights of the Hanukiyah?"

Psalms in the Key of Healing

Cantor Heinz had served a major Conservative synagogue for many years after he landed from Germany following the Second World War. He transmitted his love of Jewish music to generations of students and their families. When I met him in the nursing home, he had advanced Parkinson's disease. He could no longer walk or stand, and it was hard for him to speak. I had to strain mightily to catch his quiet words. One day when we were visiting, Cantor Heinz was trying to communicate something I could not understand. He was animated, and he stubbornly persisted. It turned out that he was trying to teach me a two-part melody. He wanted us to sing together, *"aranen, aranen, b'maaseh yadeнa, aranen"*—words from our Psalm 92, which mean: I will rejoice, I will sing of Your handiwork.

The singing was a teaching to me. If Cantor Heinz, so limited by his painful illness, could be moved to sing in gratitude as he savored life and creation, who am I to *kvetch* on a bad day, or to fail to notice miracles in my midst?

Sometimes gratitude comes as an older person looks back on the whole of their life. My late mother-in-law, Miriam, survived the Warsaw ghetto and a series of concentration camps; she endured hardship, dehumanization, and unspeakable loss. When she was near ninety, homebound and frail, she was asked how she viewed her life. She responded, "I've had a good life." She was deeply aware of the goodness she had experienced—a childhood in a loving family, a loving extended family forged with her husband and sisters, and small delights she still enjoyed —a sweet berry, a lovely outfit, a good *schmooze* with a friend.

Viktor Frankl, the existential psychoanalyst who survived Auschwitz, taught that an elder can find meaning in memory. Older people can draw on "the full granaries of the past into which they have brought the harvest of their lives: the deeds done, the loves loved and last, but not least, the sufferings they've gone through with courage and dignity." They can find meaning in "the potentialities they have actualized, the meanings they have fulfilled, the values they have realized. This richness, he said, can never be diminished…nothing and nobody can ever remove these assets from the past. (Frankl, 151) This meaning-making is possible, he maintained, even if there is hardship in the here-and-now.

Adversity

The second section of our psalm recognizes adversity:

> Wickedness flowers like grass, and evil abounds…
> I see myself beset…

Inevitably, a person who has lived a long time—even the happiest of lives—will have encountered struggle, disappointment, and hardship. Our later years will almost invariably put us face to face with shattering. We will experience loss—as we part with treasured partners, friends, and family, as well as roles we've found meaningful in career or community. We will meet limitations—as our bodily capacities make some beloved activities, or even routine ones, impossible. Financial security may wane. Time itself offers an ever-narrower horizon. Many elders in my community express disappointment that the social progress they worked hard to realize has not taken root as they had hoped. The tenacity of injustice, war, and violence have shattered long-held hopes.

Rose, 94-year-old woman I know, is no longer able to leave her apartment, and hence, unable to participate in a dynamic community organization she helped to found and run for decades. She asks, "Why am I still here?" Her answer: "I guess I am here to learn to ask for help, and to get over my pride."

It is easy to be swallowed up by "evils" or shatterings; all too often elders find themselves despairing. I have heard many frail elders say, "I'm no good to anyone. Why doesn't God just take me?" or, as one 99-year-old told me, "God don't want me, the devil don't want me neither." Despair is not inevitable, however. Its alternative is acceptance.

I asked Marty, a community leader, what it was like to be 77-years old. She told me, "I look around at my peers. As I see it, when you're my age, you have two choices: you can dwindle—narrow your interests, your activity, your curiosity —or be grateful. I choose the latter." She continued to engage passionately in community service and cultural life, until she faced a recurrence of cancer at age 81. The doctors told her that even if she pursued aggressive chemotherapy, they could buy her a few more months, at best. She said, "I'm not going to fight this—I am ready. She calmly gathered her family, one by one, gave them parting words and gifts, and entered hospice, where she died peacefully a few weeks later.

Flourishing

Our psalm suggests a vision of grounded, fruitful aging:

> If we live with integrity,
> we shall flourish like the palm-tree,
> casting shade like the cedars of Lebanon.
> Plant us in the house of the Eternal,
> let us flower in the presence of our God.

The psalmist envisions a ripe old age; living with integrity, finding shelter in the house of YHVH, the God who is past-present-future. Succor is to be found in connection across time —with one's own past; with our peoples' past.

One Shabbat Sarah, 85-years old, was given the honor of lighting the Shabbat candles in her retirement community, As she covered her eyes before saying the blessing, she said, "I remember my mother and grandmother doing this." At that moment, Sarah was not consumed by her aches and pains, or about the loss of a dear friend the week before. She was rooted in her past and felt part of the long chain of mothers, grandmothers, and daughters who had performed the sacred

126

act of lighting Shabbat candles. So, too, elders can feel a link to a future that will extend beyond their finite lives, and in which values precious to them will carry on.

The teenagers trooped into the nursing home, chatty, boisterous, and excited to see their older friends. They had been coming monthly to the home to help the elders who lived there to attend Shabbat services. Every pair of teens was assigned an older friend to bring to the chapel. During the service, they helped their friends to turn pages, sang with them, and participated in a discussion of the weekly Torah portion. After the service, as they enjoyed refreshments, their older friends blessed them, and exclaimed about their kindness. In sharing Shabbat and prayer with their young friends, the elders experienced Jewish continuity. While they would not long be around to keep the Jewish people going, they caught a glimpse of *netzah Yisrael,* the eternity of the Jewish people, which continues, *l'dor va-dor,* from generation-to-generation.

The psalm closes with an image of ripeness and fruitfulness:

> Let us bear fruit in old age;
> juicy and fresh we'll remain.
> We will affirm: God is my Rock,
> unfailing and unflawed.

How might we remain fruitful, juicy, and fresh in our aging? A 19th-century Hasidic *rebbe,* Moshe Chaim Ephraim of Sudilkov, warned against "spiritual aging [stagnation] which causes withering." Rather, he taught, "A person must renew their habits and customs in every moment." Rabbi Moshe Chaim Ephraim offers us a pathway toward this kind of rich old age. It is up to us, he suggests, to renew ourselves, to avoid stagnation. We renew ourselves by continuing to grow. An elder who believes she is still alive because there are things for her to learn embodies this spirit of renewal.

Psalms in the Key of Healing

Phyllis, a 90-year-old member of my congregation in the nursing home, was one of 15 participants in an Adult Confirmation program. The purpose of the program was to offer individuals who had never had a Bar or Bat Mitzvah to have a Jewish rite of passage. The women had mostly had no Jewish education, and the men had missed out on a Bar Mitzvah because of poverty or secular parents who rejected religion. Students came to class weekly for a year and engaged in a collective Mitzvah project. The program was to culminate with a Confirmation ceremony on Shavuot, at which each confirmand would speak about what the experience had meant to them.

Phyllis was diagnosed with cancer during the program. She received chemotherapy and got progressively weaker, but she came to class as often as she could. She volunteered to lead the Aleinu prayer at the end of the service. When the day for the ceremony arrived, we learned that Phyllis had been admitted to the hospital overnight. Knowing that she would very much want to attend, the nursing home administrator spent an hour on the phone begging the hospital to release her. As the service began, the room was packed with children, grandchildren, great-grandchildren and friends of the confirmands. They were excited, but also devastated that Phyllis was not there. Around the middle of the service, I looked up and saw the administrator, pushing Phyllis down the aisle in a reclining wheelchair. Phyllis looked weak but resplendent. She gave her speech and led the Aleinu. When she died a couple of weeks later, it was with the satisfaction that she had reached for, and achieved, a profoundly meaningful accomplishment.

This psalm takes us on a journey through key dimensions of the aging experience. It does not gloss over the challenges of growing older; it is honest, and real. Yet it offers a vision of rich and satisfying life in old age. The last lines of the psalm are a blessing for growing older. I offer them to you:

May we grow fruitful as we age,
ripe and abundant and sage.
Keep our hearts open to all we face,
present to goodness, even a trace.
Renew us, let our spirits soar.
Sustain us, Our Rock, for more."[2]

---

2. To listen to a melody for this blessing, visit *https://growingolder.net/may-we-grow-fruitful-as-we-age/*.

Psalm 103
Forgiveness

Translation and Interpretation by
Rabbi Rafael Goldstein, BCC

For David

1. Bless the Holy One, O my soul;
    all my being God's holy name.

2. Bless the Holy One, O my soul,
    and do not forget all God's kindness.

3. God forgives all your sins,
    heals all your diseases.

4. God redeems your life from the pit,
    surrounds you with steadfast love and mercy.

5. God satisfies you with good things in the prime of life,
    so that your youth is renewed like an eagle's.

6. The Holy One executes acts of justice
    and judgments for all who are wronged.

7. God's ways were made known to Moses,
    God's deeds to the children of Israel.

8. The Holy One is compassionate and gracious,
    slow to anger, abounding in steadfast love.

9. God will not contend forever
    or nurse anger for all time.

10. God has not dealt with us according to our sins,
    God has not repaid us according to our iniquities.

Psalms in the Key of Healing

11. For as the heavens are high above the earth,
    God's steadfast love is intensified
    for those who are in awe of God.
12. As east is from west, so far has God removed
    our sins from us.
13. As a parent has compassion for his/her children,
    so the Holy One has compassion
    for those who are in awe of God.
14. For God knows how we are formed;
    God is mindful that we are dust.
15. Our days are like grass;
    we bloom like a flower of the field;
16. if a wind passes over it, it is gone,
    and its site knows it no more.
17. But God's steadfast love is for all eternity
    towards those who experience the awe of God,
    and God's kindness is for the children's children
18. of those who keep the covenant
    and those who remember God's desires to fulfill them.
19. God's throne is established in heaven,
    and God's rule is over all.
20. Bless the Holy One, God's messengers,
    mighty creatures who do God's bidding,
    obey the voice of God's word.
21. Bless the Holy One, all God's workers who do God's will.
22. Bless the Holy One, all God's creatures
    in all the places where God is found;
    bless the Holy One, O my soul.

לְדָוִד ׀ בָּרְכִי נַפְשִׁי אֶת־יְהֹוָה וְכָל־קְרָבַי אֶת־שֵׁם קָדְשׁוֹ׃
בָּרְכִי נַפְשִׁי אֶת־יְהֹוָה וְאַל־תִּשְׁכְּחִי כָּל־גְּמוּלָיו׃
הַסֹּלֵחַ לְכָל־עֲוֺנֵכִי הָרֹפֵא לְכָל־תַּחֲלֻאָיְכִי׃
הַגּוֹאֵל מִשַּׁחַת חַיָּיְכִי הַמְעַטְּרֵכִי חֶסֶד וְרַחֲמִים׃
הַמַּשְׂבִּיעַ בַּטּוֹב עֶדְיֵךְ תִּתְחַדֵּשׁ כַּנֶּשֶׁר נְעוּרָיְכִי׃
עֹשֵׂה צְדָקוֹת יְהֹוָה וּמִשְׁפָּטִים לְכָל־עֲשׁוּקִים׃
יוֹדִיעַ דְּרָכָיו לְמֹשֶׁה לִבְנֵי יִשְׂרָאֵל עֲלִילוֹתָיו׃
רַחוּם וְחַנּוּן יְהֹוָה אֶרֶךְ אַפַּיִם וְרַב־חָסֶד׃
לֹא־לָנֶצַח יָרִיב וְלֹא לְעוֹלָם יִטּוֹר׃
לֹא כַחֲטָאֵינוּ עָשָׂה לָנוּ וְלֹא כַעֲוֺנֹתֵינוּ גָּמַל עָלֵינוּ׃
כִּי כִגְבֹהַּ שָׁמַיִם עַל־הָאָרֶץ גָּבַר חַסְדּוֹ עַל־יְרֵאָיו׃
כִּרְחֹק מִזְרָח מִמַּעֲרָב הִרְחִיק מִמֶּנּוּ אֶת־פְּשָׁעֵינוּ׃
כְּרַחֵם אָב עַל־בָּנִים רִחַם יְהֹוָה עַל־יְרֵאָיו׃
כִּי־הוּא יָדַע יִצְרֵנוּ זָכוּר כִּי־עָפָר אֲנָחְנוּ׃
אֱנוֹשׁ כֶּחָצִיר יָמָיו כְּצִיץ הַשָּׂדֶה כֵּן יָצִיץ׃
כִּי רוּחַ עָבְרָה־בּוֹ וְאֵינֶנּוּ וְלֹא־יַכִּירֶנּוּ עוֹד מְקוֹמוֹ׃
וְחֶסֶד יְהֹוָה ׀ מֵעוֹלָם וְעַד־עוֹלָם
עַל־יְרֵאָיו וְצִדְקָתוֹ לִבְנֵי בָנִים׃
לְשֹׁמְרֵי בְרִיתוֹ וּלְזֹכְרֵי פִקֻּדָיו לַעֲשׂוֹתָם׃
יְהֹוָה בַּשָּׁמַיִם הֵכִין כִּסְאוֹ וּמַלְכוּתוֹ בַּכֹּל מָשָׁלָה׃
בָּרְכוּ יְהֹוָה מַלְאָכָיו גִּבֹּרֵי כֹחַ
עֹשֵׂי דְבָרוֹ לִשְׁמֹעַ בְּקוֹל דְּבָרוֹ׃
בָּרְכוּ יְהֹוָה כָּל־צְבָאָיו מְשָׁרְתָיו עֹשֵׂי רְצוֹנוֹ׃
בָּרְכוּ יְהֹוָה ׀ כָּל־מַעֲשָׂיו
בְּכָל־מְקֹמוֹת מֶמְשַׁלְתּוֹ בָּרְכִי נַפְשִׁי אֶת־יְהֹוָה׃

Psalm 103—Forgiveness

Forgiveness is one of the more challenging experiences humanity faces. Most religions have a means of seeking and receiving God's forgiveness, and have concepts of repentance, atonement, and reconciliation. Judaism, Catholicism, and most Protestant denominations provide vehicles for receiving forgiveness, and all say that God is ready, willing, and able to forgive the repentant sinner.

This psalm touches on themes of illness and punishment, and theology of a compassionate, gracious God. Regret, apology, and forgiveness is the model. When we harm another person, we're supposed to ask their forgiveness. But it's the forgiving that sometimes is the hardest part. Apology is easy. The thing which was done is done: there's no way to undo it.

The psalm points out the paradigm: If God can forgive us for all the rotten things we have done, and we are supposed to be like God, we are supposed to find a way out of the bitterness and the pettiness. Yet for humanity, the act of forgiving is much more problematic. There are things people do to one another that are considered to be "unforgivable" by the person who will not or does not forgive. It's important to forgive precisely because it's not the other person who is suffering as a result of the bitterness; it's the person holding onto the bitterness. If we don't learn to forgive, all the bitterness just burns us up, and does nothing to the target of the bitterness.

According to Rabbi Harold Kushner:

> The embarrassing secret is that many of us are reluctant to forgive. We nurture grievances because they make us feel morally superior. Withholding forgiveness gives us a sense of power, often power over someone who otherwise leaves us feeling powerless. The only power we have over them is the power to remain angry at them. At some level, we enjoy the role of being the long-suffering, aggrieved party. (Kushner, 1999)

"Bless the Holy One, O my soul;
all my being God's holy name...
God forgives all your sins,
heals all your diseases."

We sing praises of God because of God's incredible capacity to forgive, no matter what; to love us, no matter what. God will forgive us, no matter what we did. In fact, God loves the sinners the most, because they are the ones who have to find a new path, a new direction, and come back to God. (I don't say this to encourage people to be sinners, whatever that means, but to assure all of us that no matter what we did, God is waiting for us to return.) This is God's kindness: God forgives us.

It is not just about God, though. It is the paradigm for all of us: If God can forgive us for what obviously must be our biggest failings, then we are supposed to be like God and forgive others the same way. We are supposed imitate God's forgiveness, to let go of our bitterness, and move beyond whatever hurt us, to rebuild our relationships with those who hurt us (intentionally or unintentionally).

Yes, there are unforgivable things that happen. For most of us, most of the time, nothing is unforgivable. I come into contact with families that are split because of something that happened or something that was said decades ago. Are they really better off completely disconnecting from people they used to love for decades? Do they even remember why they are not speaking? Maybe what was unforgivable 20 years ago can be seen in a different light, or even just let go. Maybe they could focus on everything else, and leave the elephant in the room, so it will shrink on its own.

Forgiveness sometimes does not mean reconciliation. We just don't have a word in English for the process of letting go of the anger and hurt, without necessarily reconciling. God reconciles with everyone. We don't have to; we just have to let go of the bitterness and anger. Asking for forgiveness is the easy part. Actually forgiving is the hard part.

But what does "healing all your diseases" mean in spiritual terms? How is "healing" different from "curing?" So often in the Bible we experience an angry God bringing a plague or an illness in response to sins of the people. Does God really make people sick for sinning? We have to remember the mentality and perspective of the people who wrote the Bible, even as they were divinely inspired to do so: they could only relate to God in the ways they knew. These were people who were primitive, and that gods were wrathful. They knew the only way to make God happy was through animal sacrifices. The balance to their being primitive is that they also saw God as compassionate, slow to anger, just, forgiving, loving, and caring. Since we are not so primitive and we no longer engage in animal sacrifice to worship, we also need to understand God from a different perspective.

While our ancestors believed that God punished people through illness, that is not the God we believe in. I do not believe that God is sitting around trying to figure out how to best torture me today. I do not believe that God wants bad things to happen to me, and I can find no reason to believe that one wrong thing that I did would lead to extreme personal punishment from God. What good would the punishment be if I don't know that what I did was so wrong that God has decided to punish me? Punishments have to fit crimes. If I have to guess what I did to deserve a punishment, it's not much of a lesson from God.

The worst cliché ever invented by people: God doesn't give you more than you can handle. The theology of this nonsense is awful. God neither gives people diseases nor can we handle everything that comes our way. I cannot believe in a nasty, capricious God that punishes me for reasons I don't know, or who "gives" me an illness that will kill me. This cliché also takes away my ability (or desire) to ask God for help with whatever it is I am experiencing. If God wanted me to have this, how can I ask God to help me not have it? I believe in a God of compassion and mercy, who would never work to harm me, but will help me through whatever crisis I am experiencing.

As I write this, I have multiple cancers, and I am suffering both from the illness and from the chemotherapy, which is supposed to make me feel better, and isn't.

It's not God's fault that I have cancer. It's not my fault that I have cancer. Cancer happens. The last thing I want to do is to blame God, or myself, since neither approach is particularly helpful. Would it bring me comfort to somehow believe that I got something I deserve? People do all kinds of things which might be toxic, both knowingly and unknowingly. We can't really pin serious illness on behavior, diet, exercise—or lack thereof, though they may be contributing factors. The reality is that people in terrific shape get sick; people who jog daily have heart attacks; people with perfect cholesterol still have strokes. Bad things happen. Body parts go haywire.

Life is what happens when your plans change. I served as the on-call chaplain at Sharp Memorial Hospital in San Diego on Sundays. Most of the people who came in via ambulance were in motorcycle accidents, especially when the weather was really nice. One day a man who was in terrific shape was brought in wearing jogging clothes. The doctor, who was obese, said, "See what happens when you work out? It's only the fit ones who come here with heart attacks on Sundays."

As I write this, I am also in my eighth week of isolation (due to Covid-19). I have done everything I can to not come into contact with the virus, and have anxiety attacks if I go into a store, even with a mask on. I don't believe God will give me the virus. God is not in that business. If I get it, it will be because a germ got through to me, somehow, not because I didn't go to religious services religiously (as it were), or any other behavior on my part or on the part of God. People get sick. People die. That's the natural order of the world.

Psalms in the Key of Healing

Ultimately, it's not the cure we can expect; cures can be very elusive. We can hope for cures. They depend on medical scientists and great doctors, and there will always be the next incurable illness after today's incurable illnesses are cured. But *healing* is completely different. Healing is about wholeness, comfort, and peace. Healing is spiritual, while curing is physical. One can be healed spiritually, and very ill physically. A person who is experiencing spiritual healing is more likely to find strength through his/her illness and learn to hope for that which can be real. Healing can come in the form of reconciliation, forgiveness, renewal of relationships, and a sense of purpose (bucket lists are great examples of healing). Healing can transform the experience of suffering and focus energy on that which can be achieved.

The number one priority on my bucket list is to finish this book. Everything else can wait or not happen. If I never get to go to Quebec, or Jerusalem again, so be it. I can literally live with that. But helping people see strength, hope, clarity, and healing in illness is my highest priority. That is what my life has been about and thanking God for enabling me to reach this day.

Is illness a punishment? How does punishment work without a verdict, without knowing what one did wrong? How can illness be a punishment when God is a forgiving God? Think about God's job description—it does not include punishment of people. What does it include?

I used to work in a hospital with 1,100 beds. That means that 1,100 people, just in that hospital, had done something so bad that they were being punished for it, including babies. If illness is punishment from God, then doctors and nurses should not be working to bring healing. That would be contrary to God's will. Instead of doctors and nurses and medical workers there should be guards and executioners who would then be doing God's will. The big conundrum would remain though: if you don't know what you are being punished for, what good is the punishment?

> *"God redeems your life from the pit,*
> *surrounds you with steadfast love and mercy...*
> *The Holy One executes acts of justice*
> *and judgments for all who are wronged."*

God's redemption, love, mercy, kindness and support are all there. All we have to do is see them and accept them! The pit is when we hit rock bottom, as any participant in AA or NA or other twelve-step groups can attest. When God redeems us from the pit, we surrender to God, recognize that in the pit the only way to gain control over our lives is to cede control, recognize that we are powerless over the things that bring our lives into this abyss, and turn to God to help us—redeem us.

I met with a Pentecostal bishop who was suffering extreme pain. After some introductory discussion, she said that her suffering was bringing her closer to Jesus. It helped her understand his suffering and helped her see so clearly that his suffering was for her, and she was suffering for him. She welcomed the pain, because it had unique meaning for her, and she felt she could learn from the terrible experience she was having. She found meaning and healing in the suffering.

God will renew our youth "like an eagle's" means we can take comfort in feeling youthful and bright; as strong as an eagle. Our youth is renewed even as we age—when we take flight satisfied with the love of the Holy One.

God is the judge for all who are wronged. What happens when we do not see God's judgment, or understand it? We all know good people who are suffering, and we all see people who are nasty that seem to be prospering. Where is the justice in that?

We may not see the results of God's judgments of others, but we can be confident that God judges us and forgives us. The judgments God has for other people are simply not your, or my, business. Reread the commentary on being a sheep in God's flock. If we are in God's flock, we should know our limitations and our place in the world. We don't get to judge or order our shepherd around.

> *"God's ways were made known to Moses...*
> *God has not dealt with us according to our sins;*
> *God has not repaid us according to our iniquities."*

God is compassionate and gracious—Moses and our ancestors knew it. God's steadfast love is abounding; it's not going to go away, no matter what. As any parent loves his/her child even if the parent doesn't approve of what the child has done, God loves us. God will forgive us, and whatever anger God might have toward us for disappointing God, there are no grudges. We can come back anytime (or anywhere) and find the same loving, forgiving, and gracious God. We may, in some way, have "earned" some kind of punishment, but God doesn't work that way.

God does not demand some kind of retribution for things we have done wrong. Here again is the perfect response to someone who is convinced God is punishing him/her because of something s/he has done. That's not how God works. We don't have retribution for the terrible things we do—we have opportunities for repentance and on-going love. We may think we deserve to be punished, but that is up to us. It is not going to come from God.

> *"For as the heavens are high above the earth...*
> *As a parent has compassion for his/her children,*
> *so the Holy One has compassion*
> *for those who are in awe of God."*

The Hebrew for "Awe of God" is often mistranslated as "fear" of God. Both translations are accurate, but we have nothing to fear from God. God is amazing, awesome, awe-inspiring, and unbelievably gracious to us in many ways. Why would we fear God? Think of it as if you are standing at the edge of the Grand Canyon: It's an amazing sight, but kind of scary too; a little slip and you're on your way down the cliff. While it takes your breath away to see such a sight, it's awesome and amazing, cool and frightening in some ways at the same time. The awe that we experience with regard to God is the same mix of feelings.

God's love is intensified for people who are in awe of God, not because those people deserve more love, but because they are *aware* of it. This line is often misinterpreted to mean that if you don't "fear" God you don't get God's love. It makes much more sense to note that if you are not in awe of God, you will not sense God's love, which is there and available for you.

How far is east from west? Not far at all: simple turn—a 180; a U-turn. East and west are not distant; they are, in fact, contiguous. Just turn around; just turn your gaze—there is no distance there at all. So, if God removes our sins from us as far as east is from west, God has simply enabled you to change direction, to move forward without the sense of being sinful or "bad." Doing good, repenting, and turning back to God is a small shift, as far as east is from west. All you have to do is make the turn.

How far is God's compassion from us? Can God's compassion be found even in suffering, illness, grief, and loss? How? Once again, we can call upon God and find God's compassion. But what does that mean? It does not mean a "cure" for whatever ails us; God's compassion can help us through what ails us. That compassion is ever-present, available for us. Unfortunately, so many of us confuse that concept of compassion with a cure, and once again, curing is not in God's job description. Compassion is.

"For God knows how we are formed;
God is mindful that we are dust....
But God's steadfast love is for all eternity
towards those who experience the awe of God."

While many of us build ourselves up to presume we are something much more than we are, the great equalizer is death. Compared with God the Eternal, we are nothing. Our days pass like we have no time at all. The psalmist goes beyond being sheep in God's flock (Psalm 23). In this psalm we are less than what the sheep munch on! The less we are, the more amazing it is that God cares about us; each of the blades of grass, each of the flowers in the field, and has compassion on us.

God remembers that we are dust, mere nothings in God's realm. But that also means that God remembers that we are not perfect beings. God cannot expect perfection from us. God remembering how little and insignificant we are also indicates that God has to forgive us for our frailties, our faults, and our failures. God expects us to be and to do wrong because that is how we are created. We are not gods. The expectation of us is that we will be human, and we will demonstrate that humanity regularly. God expects nothing else but for us to be who we are.

God is mindful that we are that dust, and God is surprised by what we achieve in our limited ways. Our creativity, our inventiveness, and our determination are all like blooming flowers, extreme in beauty. Even as our bodies fade, the memory of that beauty remains. We will bloom and vanish physically; wind may well erase all traces of us, but the beauty remains in memory.

God's steadfast love is forever, beyond our days. Though wind can erase our physical existence, the love lasts forever; God takes us in forever. That love is for all of us, but the people who are aware of God's love, in awe of it, are the ones who experience it. Not because others are punished—quite the opposite. You can't be in awe of something you are not aware of or deny exists.

The love is there for you even when you don't know it.

The love is there, but there is no quid pro quo: love God back or not, it's your choice. God will continue loving you, seeing your unique value, and your beauty, whether you are in awe of God or not. To feel God's love: love. To feel God's forgiveness: forgive. To feel God's compassion: have compassion. To feel God's presence: be present.

"...and God's kindness is for the children's children
of those who keep the covenant...
God's throne is established in heaven,
and God's rule is overall."

All of us want the next generation to have a better life than we have had. But again we have that caveat, for "those who keep the covenant." For people who don't keep the covenant, do their grandchildren suffer? First, we need to define "keep the covenant." The terminology is pretty broad, and it's not clear how one "keeps the covenant." Some might say: obey the Ten Commandments.

But that is the very least you can do. Is not murdering really such an achievement? Most, if not all of us, probably will not murder, kidnap, lie under oath, or break most of the other commandments. The text is vague here for a reason: to enable all of us to qualify, in one way or another, as people who keep the covenant. We can do it in a minimalist way by simply recognizing our heritage, or in a maximalist way by observing every possible commandment and then some. The vagueness of this phrase is intended to make us all people who keep the covenant. God's kindness will be felt by all of our future generations.

When you put that together with the recognition that we are mere blades of grass—flowers that wither and fade—it should bring comfort to know that God's kindness extends beyond our lifetimes, to generations to come. Somehow these blades of grass add up in a multigenerational experience of God's kindness.

Again, "those who remember to fulfill God's desires," is very vague to be inclusive of everyone. God's desires are both known and unknowable. We have the concept of *mitzvot* (acts of commandment), often mistranslated as good deeds. *Mitzvot* are their own reward. Doing good does not earn anyone points for the world to come, but rather gives us opportunities to feel, experience, and know God's desires. In the moment one does a mitzvah, one receives the benefit of knowing s/he has done something good and that knowledge is its own reward. If you don't do it, or don't recognize that you did it, the reward is still there, but you miss out on knowing about it.

God reigns over all, according to the psalmist: over the sinner and the saint, over the true believer and the doubter, over all that exists. God ruling over us brings us security and strength in touching a piece of that eternity, connecting with that which is way beyond us. Whether we are flowers, blades of grass or dust, we are a part of that realm; we are a part of something incredibly awesome.

> *"Bless the Holy One, God's messengers,*
> *mighty creatures who do God's bidding,*
> *obey the voice of God's word...*
> *bless the Holy One, O my soul."*

How does blessing the Holy One work? Does God need our blessings? Every time we say a blessing, we recognize the partnership between God and humanity. When we say a blessing over bread, we say "Holy One of Blessing, your Presence fills the Universe, you bring forth bread from the ground." Obviously loaves of bread do not grow from the ground, but the blessing affirms that growth of any kind is partnership—raw materials— and what we do with them that we are grateful for.

God doesn't need our blessings: we do. We need to be regularly reminded that we are in a partnership with God to make the world a better place, to complete God's acts of creation. God depends on us to make creation meaningful. In the first story of creation in the Bible (not science or history, the creations stories are allegories to teach us theology), God creates all things so that they can procreate. Trees and vegetation are all seed-bearing; fish, birds, animals, and people are created with the expectation that they will procreate. The only thing that was created without the ability to procreate was Shabbat. The only way for Shabbat to happen is if people make it by observing Shabbat. Partnership.

When we say bless God, what we are really saying is "bless this partnership." We will do our job in response to the wonders You have done for us. Blessings are reminders of our bounty, reminders of how lucky and "blessed" we are by God. Blessings are expressions of gratitude, awareness of the blessings in one's own life.

Pulling It All Together

If God can forgive (and that is the paradigm), what are the implications when there are irreconcilable differences between people? Unforgivable? Ultimately, this psalm is here to say that God sees nothing as unforgivable, and therefore we cannot. While we do not have an obligation to reconcile, God does. We just need to let go of the anger and see what else can happen for us, not for the person who has done something we cannot forgive. But we should always be asking whether the thing we are so angry about, that hurt us so much, is worth the loss of companionship, love, friendship, or family. Does it remain unforgivable for the remainder of one's life, or is there a way to step around it and actually relate to one another once again?

If someone can't be communicated with, or continues to do things that are offensive, there is no obligation to allow him/her to continue to do damage. But how good does the other person have to be? Can one find the love in the other places and keep away from the sore spots? Can people agree to disagree and yet maintain a relationship of love and respect?

Illness is not a punishment from God. God is compassionate, merciful, just, kind. Attributing an illness to God without knowing what "sin" the punishment is for makes God anything but just. God doesn't give us that which is bad for us. God is there to help us through the bad, difficult, horrible, intolerable experiences we may have. God is our ongoing, permanent resource for finding the blessings which we may not be able to find in suffering or sadness.

Psalm 121
Hope (Perspective)

Translation and Interpretation by
Rabbi Rafael Goldstein, BCC

A song to the heights
1. I lift up my eyes to the mountains
      From where will my help come?
2. My help comes from the Holy One,
      Maker of heaven and earth.
3. God will not let your foot give way;
      Your guardian will not slumber.
4. See the Guardian of Israel
      neither slumbers nor sleeps.
5. The Holy One is your guardian,
      your protection at your right hand.
6. By day, the sun will not strike you,
      nor the moon by night.
7. The Holy One will guard you from all that is bad.
      The Holy One will guard your spirit.
8. The Holy One will guard
      your going and coming now and forever.

שִׁ֗יר לַֽמַּ֫עֲל֥וֹת אֶשָּׂ֣א עֵ֭ינַי אֶל־הֶהָרִ֑ים מֵ֝אַ֗יִן יָבֹ֥א עֶזְרִֽי׃
עֶ֭זְרִי מֵעִ֣ם יְהוָ֑ה עֹ֝שֵׂ֗ה שָׁמַ֥יִם וָאָֽרֶץ׃
אַל־יִתֵּ֣ן לַמּ֣וֹט רַגְלֶ֑ךָ אַל־יָ֝נ֗וּם שֹֽׁמְרֶֽךָ׃
הִנֵּ֣ה לֹֽא־יָ֭נוּם וְלֹ֣א יִישָׁ֑ן שׁ֝וֹמֵ֗ר יִשְׂרָאֵֽל׃
יְהוָ֥ה שֹׁמְרֶ֑ךָ יְהוָ֥ה צִ֝לְּךָ֗ עַל־יַ֥ד יְמִינֶֽךָ׃
יוֹמָ֗ם הַשֶּׁ֥מֶשׁ לֹֽא־יַכֶּ֗כָּה וְיָרֵ֥חַ בַּלָּֽיְלָה׃
יְהוָ֗ה יִשְׁמָרְךָ֥ מִכָּל־רָ֑ע יִ֝שְׁמֹ֗ר אֶת־נַפְשֶֽׁךָ׃
יְהוָ֗ה יִשְׁמָר־צֵֽאתְךָ֥ וּבוֹאֶ֑ךָ מֵֽ֝עַתָּ֗ה וְעַד־עוֹלָֽם׃

Psalm 121 Hope (Everything and its Opposite)

Psalm 121 speaks about our desire to be protected, sheltered, and cared for, much the way a sheep might be protected in Psalm 23. Yet a careful reading of the psalm leads to a much more nuanced sense of perspective: no matter where one stands, there is a way to see and frame a sense of hope.

There is no such thing as a hopeless situation. There are only situations in which people have lost track of what they can hope for. Hope doesn't have to be for physical recovery, cure, or resolution. Hope can be establishing goals, thoughts, anything to lead to something better. We don't have to like the reality of being human, but once we begin to accept our own humanity with some humility, we can then deal with hope, within the natural order of the world. Hope is an expectation that somehow something good will happen. It is the belief that we have some control or influence over a situation. Hope is reframing of experience to include other possibilities.

A song to the heights
I lift up my eyes to the mountains
From here will my help come?
My help comes from the Holy One,
Maker of heaven and earth.

148

A song to the heights? Psalm 121 is the only psalm with this introduction; the others are songs *of* the heights. This seems to imply that it is intended to sing as one goes to the heights, not when one gets there. But where is the psalmist coming from, and where is s/he going?

Where is the psalmist standing? Most people would say in a valley, looking up at the mountains. Is that the only possibility? I remember standing in Olympic National Park on top of a mountain, lifting my eyes and seeing all the other mountains surrounding where I was standing. I don't know whether the outlook I was standing on was higher or lower than the distant mountains, I just remember lifting my eyes to the mountains, and I was not necessarily beneath them. Here we have the first element of everything and its opposite in this psalm: Are we looking from below or are we looking from above? I lift my eyes to the mountains leads me to immediately say "I am looking for perspective."

The mountains also lead me to questions. What does a mountain mean to us? For many of us, mountains are opportunities for an incredible view, if we are on top. For many mountains symbolize challenges, the "insurmountable" if we are beneath. For many they conjure up fresh air, since many of us picture verdant mountains and not glaciers. When some people see mountains, they gain a sense of awe, feel closer to nature, wonder at how these natural wonders came into being, or sense appreciation for their existence.

Mountains can be places of refuge, and they can also be places of exile. Mountains can be sources of hope. The Messiah is supposed to come down from the mountains. The Messiah is our greatest source of hope, and with his arrival the world will become a place of peace and goodness. The mountain could be a symbol of the Messiah, and anticipation that everything will change for the better. So perhaps this psalmist is implying the hope that s/he is looking to the mountains to see the greatest source of hope: the Messiah. But hope coming from the

149

experience of mountains is not so foreign. Even in David's time, mountains were the easiest places to defend and the hardest places to attack. Being in the mountains would be a source of feeling strength and hope.

Mountains can also symbolize the world. They represent that which we can see as huge, from whatever point of view we look at a mountain. Compared with mountains, we are indeed small, almost insignificant. But in observing them, we are also seeing ourselves as part of a greater whole—a world that includes both people and mountains, small and large.

As a Jewish person from the New York area, and growing up when I did, the Catskill Mountains were a source of comfort and joy in summertime. They were cooler because of their altitude, close enough to the city to escape to them for weekends. Many other cities have had summer mountain refuges.

"I lift my eyes to the mountains" may well mean "I am looking for hope, refuge." The mountains may symbolize perspective as well. Lifting my eyes can be looking forward, looking down (as in looking out from one mountain to another which happens to be lower), or looking up, all in search of hope. One can truly gain perspective gazing at the mountains. The mere physicality of the mountain may provide perspective or the sense of oneself in comparison to the world.

"From where will my help come?"

The assumption one immediately has is that the answer to this question is in the next line: from the Holy One. But why ask such a question if the answer is so obvious? Is it indeed so obvious? The word in Hebrew, *mei'ayin,* does mean "from where." But it also means "from nothing." *Ayin* is "nothingness." In other words, it may not be such an obvious question, but could be an affirmative statement: My help comes from nothingness.

How does help come from nothingness? Nothingness could mean "from nothing," as in, from "no thing." This could be one way to describe God—no thing. My help comes from an awesome, awe-ful being that is no thing, nothing we can understand. We cannot see, touch, or feel God. While we might not feel comfortable thinking of God as nothing, no thing, but when you think about it, it is true. When help comes from God it comes from no thing. Belief in God, a belief in that which we can't touch or see is an act of faith in that which is beyond us, not a thing.

But the opposite is also true: "nothing" could refer to humanity. My help may come from people; but, as we saw in Psalm 103, people are like flowers that wither and are gone. If I am looking to other people for my help, I am looking for help from mortal beings who have nothing and long-term are nothing. Great doctors and nurses, great researchers, great chaplains are all temporary. If I am looking for help from humanity, I am looking for help from no thing. (While saying people do the best they can, which is actually something. We have to remember the psalmist's perspective which goes beyond generations.)

The other question that has to be asked is "what help?" Why is the psalmist first and foremost looking for help in this psalm? What does the psalmist need help with? While all of us could use some help, it's usually not the first thing we consider: most of us would attempt to take care of ourselves first and seek help when we have exhausted our own resources. So, is the psalmist in the throes of despair, having tried, exhausted all other options, and now ready to turn to the Holy One as a last resort? Has the psalmist "reached bottom?" Is the psalmist surrendering to the Holy One?

There are times in all of our lives when we seek help. From childhood we learn to try to solve problems ourselves, but we also learn to turn to others when we can't do it alone. Many of us have difficulty admitting we can't and are ashamed when we ask for help. Yet many of us also go into helping professions because we know two heads are better than one, and involving helpers in our problems may give us new ideas and new perspectives. We come across all kinds of challenges that may feel like they are beyond us. Certainly, serious illness, unexpected relationship entanglements, relationships with loved ones, employment challenges, and a myriad of other life events may lead us to seek help. We seek help from other people, often professionals or experts in their fields; we seek help from that which is beyond us, often when all else fails.

When we ask for help from other people, most of the time they do whatever they can to help us. But when that help is inadequate is when we ask, "Where will my help come from?" or say "I'll surrender to God" for help. Sometimes seeking help is really about seeking the strength, to do for ourselves, that which we would prefer to have a *deus ex machina* do for us by magic. Sometimes help comes in the form of understanding that there are some things which are beyond our abilities to change, and that there are some things that we can change easily.

When we "surrender" to God, we are reciting the Serenity prayer: "God, grant me the serenity to accept the things I cannot change, the courage to change the things I can, and the wisdom to know the difference." In this prayer, by surrendering, we are letting go of the things we cannot change (instead of focusing on them and getting nowhere). Most of the time, when we focus on the things we cannot change, we are simply banging our heads against the wall. Any time we are asking "Why?," we are focused on things we cannot change. The psalmist has reached bottom and is letting go of his/her sense of control over everything.

The Book of Lamentations has five chapters in it, and it mourns the destruction of the temple in Jerusalem. Three of the chapters begin with the word *aiha* which is derived from the word *aih*, which translates as "how." Jeremiah is the author, and his approach to mourning is to ask not "why" but "how." How do we go from here? How do we survive? Instead of focusing on why the destruction happened, he points to the useful step of how do we go on? "Why" leads to more "whys," and no action.

"How" is all about action. "Why" focuses on what we cannot change, while "how" focuses on what we can do.

My help comes from the Holy One. How does that work? There was a flood, and the waters gathered outside a man's home. When the water covered his street, a rowboat came by with someone telling him to get in. The man said "God will rescue me" and waved the rowboat on. When the water reached above the first floor of his house, he stood by the windows when a National Guard boat came by. He waved it on: God will rescue me. Standing on his roof when the water rose to completely submerge his house, a helicopter came by and lowered its ladder for him. He waved it on: God will rescue me. He drowned. On his arrival in heaven he asked God what happened. God replied, "I sent a rowboat, the National Guard and the helicopter."

When my help comes from the Holy One, it is most likely delivered by people doing God's work with their own hands. Since biblical times, God has worked with the assistance of people. Why did God need Moses, or any of the prophets? Because without people in between we would actually think that our help comes from nothing; nowhere. How would we know God is involved at all? The partnership between God and humanity which was mentioned in previous chapters is very clear here: My help comes from the Holy One, Maker of Heaven and Earth, with the partnership of humanity doing God's work with our own hands.

> *"God will not let your foot give way;*
> *Your guardian will not slumber.*
> *See the Guardian of Israel*
> *neither slumbers nor sleeps."*

"God will not let your foot give way" is a reminder from Psalm 23: "God guides me in Circles of Justice / As befits God's name." We can rely upon God to be our firm foundation, to keep us from tripping on our journey. Letting your foot give way is more than physical tripping, though. It also means that God will not let you lose track of your foundation, even in hard times. We are all grounded in beliefs and the things which make us who we are. God will not let us lose that foundation.

Our guardian is on the job of taking care of us at all times, even when normal guardians might fall asleep. "Slumber" is the light sleep of someone who dozes, like a security guard at a front gate; "sleeping" is deeper. While no one expects security guards to doze off, we all know that is one of the risks of the job. Human security is frail and dozes. We all know as well that sleep, while necessary, can be a time of extreme vulnerability. When we doze little things might wake us up; when we sleep, we are much more likely to stay asleep through all kinds of potential dangers.

Sleep also serves as a metaphor for death. We put beloved dogs "to sleep" when we euthanize them. Sometimes really poor explanations of death are "big sleep." We refer to the grave as "eternal rest". Every time an anesthesiologist puts me "to sleep" for a procedure, I wonder whether I will wake up, since many TV shows often depict that moment as a person's last moment of consciousness.

If God neither slumbers nor sleeps, it means we are always secure, always being watched over. We can rely on the eternity of God. There is no point at which God is unavailable to us because God is unconscious, snoozing, or on vacation. We can rely on the eternity of God's Presence. But if we remember that God dwells within us (Psalm 27) as well as outside of us, we also can rely on that Presence in us at all times of our lives. As long as we live, we are connected to that Presence, even when *we* slumber and sleep. God will not leave us because of our humanity and need to be "off-line" for 30% of our lifetimes.

*"The Holy One is your guardian,
your protection at your right hand.
By day, the sun will not strike you,
nor the moon by night."*

The Holy One is protection at your right hand. The right hand is seen as one's dominant hand (sorry people who are left-handed). Your protection at your right hand would mean your strongest, most readily available protection.

We don't usually worry about the sun or moon striking us, but the image of the world in the ancient Near East was very different. Everyone knew that the world was flat; it had four corners, and a dome over the top. The dome was called a firmament which kept the waters above it from falling on the Earth. The Hebrew for sky is *shamayim (sham,* "there is" and *mayim,* "water"). Above whatever the firmament is, there is water. On all four sides of the Earth, there is also water, so it's like an ice cube floating in water.

The sun and the moon and the stars are decorations in the sky. They have nothing much to do with day or night. The sun decorates the day, which would be there anyway. Remember in the first creation allegory (not science or history, the creation stories are theology) God creates light and days on the first day, but the sun and moon and stars in day four. The moon and stars are decorations in the night sky.

By day the sun will not strike you now becomes a clearer image. The sun will not fall from the sky, nor the moon at night. Despite their decorative nature, they are not going to hurt you because there is a natural order to the mysteries of the world. These decorations will not fall. They will keep going on their mysterious journeys in the dome of the sky. As we can rely on our guardian to neither slumber nor sleep, we can rely on the sun and moon and stars to remain in their places and cause us no harm, because because there is a natural order to things, even if we don't understand it.

Light or dark do affect us though. Many of us have fears of darkness. We prefer to be in the light, to be able to see where we are going and what we are doing. We may be comforted by light, and feel discomfort in darkness. This assurance of day and night being consistent, and reliable, means we do not need to fear the dark times (when most of us sleep, and can rely on God to not sleep). We have many expressions about being left in the dark, and finding the light. We associate good with light and difficult with dark. We also associate indecisiveness and worry with gray areas, being in the shadows. We talk about dark times in our lives, and times when we bask in sunshine. The sun and moon not striking us means that either light nor darkness, or anything in-between, should not frighten us.

"The Holy One will guard you from all that is bad.
The Holy One will guard your spirit.
The Holy One will guard
your going and coming now and forever."

The Holy One will guard you from all that is bad. The Hebrew, as in Psalm 23, of *ra* is "bad," not "evil," which has intentional connotations of "harm" and implies physical or material consequences. As in Psalm 23, one has to wonder about the traditional translations of *ra* here. Why is it usually translated "evil" in Psalm 23, and "harm" here? There is no difference in the Hebrew!

But people experience bad things all the time. If we look again at Psalm 27, we are protected by God in God's *sukkah* on a bad day, and the question of the quality of shelter in a *sukkah* was raised there. It's not physical protection, but the spiritual protection of not having to be afraid of the bad things that will inevitably happen (Psalm 23 as well). Here, the Holy One guarding us from all that is bad goes a little further. It's not just that bad things won't happen: they will happen, but we can find a way to hope through that which we may initially see as bad

—to see 'bad" in different perspectives until it is no longer so bad. Here the challenge seems to be to find the blessings hidden inside the curses.

The previous lines of this psalm have led to questions of each concept, and its opposite. Where are we standing when we lift up our eyes to the mountains: above, below, or on an even footing with the mountains at which we look? Help comes from nothing or everything—from God. God, who appears as nothing (or from people who are equal to nothing); God who is part of everything, especially us; people who are doing God's work with their own hands and are therefore not nothing. Mountains can be mountains, or they can be symbols of the arrival of the Messiah (hope). This psalm is everything and its opposite.

God will guard me from all that is bad by enabling me to have perspective, to put my mind in tune with the possibilities which may be there. Bad things will happen, but how I respond to them is all that matters, and I can respond in innumerable ways. Our most potent help, coming from God (nothingness), or humanity, is help for us to find our way through the bad. Our help is not in a cure, renewed riches, or winning lottery tickets, but in the perspective that enables us to see beyond that which we are experiencing.

In other words, God helps us through the difficult (bad) times by enabling us to see hope. Hope comes in many forms, and is the essential element to God's protection. Hope is the only antidote for despair, though when we are feeling despair, we can rarely find that hope. God helps us find the hope or helps us find the people in our lives who can shift us from despair to hope; from darkness to light.

What is hope? It is an expectation that somehow, something good will happen. Hope is a desire for something to happen or change; to have some control or influence over any situation.

There is no such thing as a hopeless situation. There are only situations in which people have lost track of what they can hope for. Hope can be establishing goals, thoughts, or anything that might lead to something better.

According to Dr. Jerome Groopman in *The Anatomy of Hope:*

- Hope is clear-eyed: Hope can be realistic, within the natural order of the world. Hope can be very practical.
- There is false hope/true hope. (False hope ignores the natural order of the world and is based on ideas that are contrary to that order.)
- Everyone has the right to hope. No matter the situation, no matter if the hope looks like denial to others, everyone has a right to hope, and our job as caring people is to help expand the horizons of hope.
- Step by step hope. Sometimes just hoping for small things, small steps instead of looking at big, overwhelming pictures may be the best expression of hope.
- Hope never dies. We actually pass it along to others. the parameters may change, but hope is a constant that we get to give away and receive. (Groopman, 2004)

What can a person hope for when life is threatened? What's real and what makes some sense:
- less pain and suffering,
- increased strength, appetite, courage,
- increased ability to share, talk and connect
- peace and comfort,
- less to worry about,
- a release from tension fear or anger,
- to be heard and to be understood,
- comfort in the world to come
- that loved ones find daily reminders of their relationships and the good times they shared,
- reconciliation of relationships, including family and friends,

• and greater awareness of God's protection, love, and support.

Once again, one can hope for the serenity to accept the things one cannot change, the courage to change what one can, and the wisdom to know the difference.

That's not to ignore miracles and unexplained recoveries. They are things to be celebrated, but not relied upon. God doesn't take orders from us (see Psalm 23), and while we can put in a request for a miracle, we have to move forward as though it might not happen. Some of the most difficult experiences I had in the Neurosurgical ICU were when families decided the only option was a miracle for their brain-dead loved one. This hunt for a miracle usually just extended suffering and led to both theological crises and disappointment. People don't "earn" miracles by living their lives according to God's laws: doing that which is right in life is its own reward. We don't walk old people across the street because we expect to be rewarded. We do it because it's the right thing to do, and we feel good in doing it.

The Holy One will guard you from all that is bad and guard your spirit by enabling you to have perspective, to reframe and rethink, and to find the hope necessary to see you through your crises. There is no better way to guard us or our spirits—lighting for us a path through the Valley of the Shadow of Death.

Most people think they know the story of Pandora's box. Everyone knows she opened it and things escaped. But what was in there? The box contained all human blessings. They all escaped, except for one: Hope.

"The Holy One will guard your going and coming, now and forever."

Americans usually think of the phrase as coming and going; why would this be backwards in our perspective? Is there a qualitative difference? If God guards your coming and going, it does not say much about where you are arriving from, or for that matter, where you are going. The phrase is pretty finite. God guards you when you show up, and when you leave.

If we look at going and coming, we are always in a state of going. We are here one minute and somewhere else the next. We are always moving on from where we are now—always in a state of going, but we don't arrive; we rarely reach our destinations. We get there when we stop going—when we die. In the meantime, God is protecting us in all our goings, in our entire life, until we arrive in a place where God's protection is eternal, now and forever.

Pulling It All Together

Have some perspective, since it can lead in very different directions. God is protecting our going until we arrive at the end of our walk through the Valley of the Shadow of Death. In the meantime, hope is what we get to live on, to experience, to thrive on. Hope is not always for the obvious, and our job as companions for others walking in this valley is to help expand the horizons of hope, to bring perspective to suffering and help enable people to find their hope. We pass hope along, sharing hope to never let it die.

Psalm 137
A Road Map for Navigating Trauma

Translation and Interpretation by
Cantor Rabbi Dr. Rhoda Harrison

1. By the rivers of Babylon, there we sat and wept aloud
       as we remembered Zion.
2. In the midst of her willow trees,
       we hung up our lyres;
3. For there our captors asked us,
       [for] words of song.
       Mocking us, our plunderers demanded joy:
       "Sing for us from Zion's songs!
4. How can we sing the Song of Adonai on foreign soil?
5. Should I forget you, Jerusalem,
       may my right hand whither;
6. May my tongue cleave to my palate,
       if I do not remember you,
       if I do not set Jerusalem above my chief joy.
7. Remember, Adonai, the Edomites
       [who] on the day of Jerusalem, said:
       "Uncover her, strip her to her foundation."
8. Daughter of Babylon the despoiler—
       Happy who pays you back in kind

for what you did to us.

9. Happy who seizes and smashes

your infants against the rock.

(Alter, 2007; 473; Freedman, 1980,

303-21; Dahood, 1966, 101-150;

and Ahn, 2008, 267-89)

עַל נַהֲרוֹת | בָּבֶל שָׁם יָשַׁבְנוּ גַּם־בָּכִינוּ בְּזָכְרֵנוּ אֶת־צִיּוֹן:

עַל־עֲרָבִים בְּתוֹכָהּ תָּלִינוּ כִּנֹּרוֹתֵינוּ:

כִּי שָׁם שְׁאֵלוּנוּ שׁוֹבֵינוּ דִּבְרֵי־שִׁיר

וְתוֹלָלֵינוּ שִׂמְחָה שִׁירוּ לָנוּ מִשִּׁיר צִיּוֹן:

אֵיךְ נָשִׁיר אֶת־שִׁיר־יְהֹוָה עַל אַדְמַת נֵכָר:

אִם־אֶשְׁכָּחֵךְ יְרוּשָׁלָם תִּשְׁכַּח יְמִינִי:

תִּדְבַּק־לְשׁוֹנִי | לְחִכִּי אִם־לֹא אֶזְכְּרֵכִי

אִם־לֹא אַעֲלֶה אֶת־יְרוּשָׁלַם עַל רֹאשׁ שִׂמְחָתִי:

זְכֹר יְהֹוָה | לִבְנֵי אֱדוֹם אֵת יוֹם יְרוּשָׁלָם

הָאֹמְרִים עָרוּ | עָרוּ עַד הַיְסוֹד בָּהּ:

בַּת־בָּבֶל הַשְּׁדוּדָה

אַשְׁרֵי שֶׁיְשַׁלֶּם־לָךְ אֶת־גְּמוּלֵךְ שֶׁגָּמַלְתְּ לָנוּ:

אַשְׁרֵי | שֶׁיֹּאחֵז וְנִפֵּץ אֶת־עֹלָלַיִךְ אֶל־הַסָּלַע:

Remembering This Psalm

When I was a young camper at the then UAHC (Union of American Hebrew Congregations, now URJ, Union for Reform Judaism) Camp Harlam in the mid-1970's, one of my favorite songs among the many we sang during our regular song sessions was a short, lyrical canon:

By the waters, the waters of Babylon
We lay down and wept, and wept for thee, Zion
We remember, thee remember,
thee remember thee Zion.

This composition "By the Waters of Babylon" was published in 1786. It was written as a sacred canon for the church by Phillip Hayes (Hayes: 1786, 105).. *The Muses Delight: Catches, Glees, Canzonets, and Canons.* London: 1786, 105. It was popularized in America after being arranged by Lee Hays for The Weavers in the mid-20th century. It was recorded by Don McLean on his 1971 album, *American Pie.* Interesting, the melody was also published in Hebrew in a 1947 German compilation of Zionist pioneer songs titled, *Shirei Eretz Yisrael.*)

What I loved most about this song was how the three parts weaved together to create a soothing metaphor for those flowing waters of Babylon and the waves of grief we all have experienced. Mind you, I had no real sense of what these waters of Babylon looked like. In my preteen years I was far from well-traveled, so the image that came to mind as a child singing this song was the Atlantic coast with waves rolling in and out along the shoreline. While my experience of grief and loss (thankfully) were also pretty limited, I still felt a visceral connection between the music with the simple layers of its canon and how it felt to grapple with sadness and tears. Even as a child, I was moved by the ability of music and text to work together to offer something more powerful than the letters written on the page. It is no wonder I became a Cantor.

The next time I encountered Psalm 137 was while reading the Hebrew Bible in preparation for those Cantorial studies at the Hebrew Union College–Jewish Institute of Religion, or as best known by its acronym, HUC. I still remember coming across the text and recognizing those opening words from that beloved camp song. As I kept reading, I recognized another very familiar set of verses, "If I forget you, O Jerusalem, let my right hand whither; let my tongue stick to my palate, if I cease to think of you"(JPS). I recognized these verses. They were as familiar as chicken soup. I knew them certainly from a piece of artwork that hung in my grandparent's home.

But I felt sure I came across these words elsewhere—maybe from my years attending synagogue services? Were they in the prayer book? Did we sing them? Or, maybe they were on a print that hung in the halls of the building? I couldn't quite pinpoint where I had come across them, but these words were engraved in my psyche. I knew they reflected a deep love and commitment to Israel, even if I didn't fully grasp why—of all curses to imagine befalling him if he forgot Jerusalem—it would be the rendering of his hand or mouth as useless that the poet put to paper. Until this moment, however, I had never connected this textual excerpt to the words I had sung at camp. How remarkable, I thought to myself, that this one nine-verse psalm would be compelling to both musical and visual artists and provide such enduring Jewish cultural touch-points.

The End of the Psalm?

Then I got to the end of the psalm. Wow. Bam. Punch. These final verses were completely unfamiliar and felt, at first glance, outrageously out of character. These verses were—they are— angry, abhorrent, and violent, leaving the reader in a state of shock. Not knowing enough about the history of the Ancient Near East or Late Antiquity (recall, this reading was in preparation for my graduate studies), I had no real context in which to place these verses. They felt completely alien to my understanding of what a Psalm, a sacred poem, should express. They challenged my respect for Biblical tradition and my Jewish identity. How could such vitriolic words, attributed to an author held up by tradition as among my Israelite ancestors, be part of the religious canon?

In practice, most of us don't have occasion to encounter the entirety of Psalm 137. The only place the recitation of the entire text of Psalm 137 is deemed obligatory in Jewish practice is just before *Birkat Hamazon* (the Blessing after Meals), on non-festival weekdays. However, only the most traditionally observant Jews recite a full *Birkat Hamazon* on weekdays. On Shabbat, when more of the Jewish community may be inclined to recite *Birkat Hamazon,* Psalm 137 is replaced by the more joyous and far more familiar Psalm 126. When Psalm 137 is used in Jewish worship, it is generally included as a prayer to express our longing for Jerusalem, and it rarely, if ever, appears in full. Examples of occasions when Jews will include selected verses from Psalm 137 in a service is on *Tishah B'Av,* the day Jews mark the fall and destruction of Jerusalem, *Yom HaZikaron,* Israel's Memorial Day, or *Yom HaAtzmaut,* Israel's Independence Day.

The last verses simply make us too uncomfortable. They unsettle us to our core. Yes, we want to remember Jerusalem, but we certainly don't want to be party to the idea of smashing babies. We are not alone. The Anglican and Catholic Church both have omitted the final three verses of Psalm 137 from their liturgical books. When it comes to our liturgy, we all seem content to follow the admonition of the Protestant German Biblical scholar, Hermann Gunkel, who wrote, "The modern mind has found in [the Bible] so much that is alien and even repellent that we have long been compelled to make selections for use in school and church and home."(Hays, 2005, 36)

I'd argue that the very fact these verses make us so viscerally uncomfortable should compel us to look at them squarely and strive to understand them within the context of history and the context of the full psalm. Life is often uncomfortable. Disappointment and pain are part of the broad complex of the human condition. Who among us hasn't faced some crisis, trial, or bereavement? Indeed, I write this chapter in the midst of a global pandemic when so many of us—our communities, our families, ourselves—are facing unprecedented loss. We don't have the option of omitting the rough moments, the painful events from our experience of living. We do, however, have the option of striving to find healing through our pain.

Psalms in the Key of Healing

Note I said "through" and not "despite." Psalm 137 offers a compelling window into the tender process of finding one's footing in the world after the experience of trauma. It doesn't ignore the pain of that trauma; on the contrary, it feels it profusely. It doesn't force a timeline on one's grief; rather, it offers a resting place, not just by the waters of Babylon but literally sandwiched between Psalms of Praise (i.e., Psalms 136 and 138), for the full recognition and experience of heartache.

As Joshua R. R. Garcia, in describing the disorientation [3]presented in Psalm 137, writes that Psalm 137 provides,"an example of an intensely raw phase in the process of healing..." (Garcia, 2002, 44) I'd argue further that Psalm 137 offers more than an example of that "intensely raw phase" of grief but also provides a window into many sides of grief. Elisabeth Kübler-Ross, in her ground-breaking work on grief, *On Death And Dying*, (Kubler-Ross, 1970, 45-48) reminds us that there is no correct way to grieve. She teaches us from the start that those now well-known five stages she outlined (denial, anger, bargaining, depression, and acceptance) are less predictable, linear steps to climb and far more places we inhabit as we travel in and out of them throughout the healing journey (Ibid., 45-48) The goal in managing grief is at its best a task in learning to integrate our experience of trauma in a way that allows us to live with it as we strive to move forward through this journey we call life.

As we will come back to at the end of this chapter, the placement of Psalm 137 within the canon of the Psalms is as important as the nine verses themselves. The final editor of our book of Psalms was furthering a valuable lesson. The book of Psalms does not conclude with Psalm 137. We don't have to remain in that "intensely raw phase" of illness, loss, or crisis. We have the capacity to move forward through our darkest

---

3 Garcia credits Walter Brueggemann with the term "disorientation" (Brueggeman, 2002, p. 44)

moments to a place of wholeness; we can reconcile our grief with the experience of joy and gratitude.

Those words I grew up singing, at camp with that 19th century melody made famous by the Weavers, provide the *sitz und leben,* the geographic and social context, to our psalm. This is a moment of incredible pain and trauma for the community. While dating is generally less than clear with most psalm texts, the opening verses of Psalm 137 place it firmly in the first half of the sixth century BCE, during the period when the Babylonians razed Jerusalem (Friedman, 318-19; Ahn, 268-74). This was a period of turmoil, trauma, and war. Jerusalem was not just a place the Israelites lived, it was the epicenter of their identity, a place that served as both temporal and religious center. Its fall was crushing physically, emotionally, and spiritually.

Psalm 137's author was most certainly a first-hand witness to the horror of destruction and conquest as well as the physical disorientation of displacement:

By the rivers of Babylon, there
we sat and wept aloud as we remembered Zion.
In the midst of her willow trees, we hung up our lyres;
For there our captors had asked us,[for] words of song.
Mocking us, our tormentors demanded joy:
'Sing for us from Zion's songs!'

Here the survivors, quite possibly a group of the Levitical Temple musicians, mourn their loss, crying aloud, and hanging up the beloved tools of their trade, while their captors continue to taunt them. The mockery is heard in the Hebrew: *tolinu* (hung up), *shoveinu* (our captors), *tolaleinu* (our tormentors), the alliteration furthering the mockery and the subsequent pain and disillusionment felt by those mourners on the shore. John Ahn suggests that these captors and tormentors (the *shoveinu* and *tolaleinu*) represent two distinct groups of antagonists; the former representing the Babylonian captors themselves and the latter representing a group already subjugated into work by the Babylonians (Ahn, 282). Not only are those who destroyed their home goading them into song, but others, victims from whom we might expect some solace and compassion, are also ridiculing these new exiles. We can almost feel their mocking taunts—"where's your God now?"—in their provocations to sing "from Zion's songs."

The simple response underscores the anguish, the humiliation, the dislocation "How can we sing the Song of Adonai on foreign soil?" When we are in the depths of a crisis, how can we sing the song of Adonai? A number of years ago, I lost a very close friend and musical companion to suicide. It was, of course, sudden, shocking, and disorienting. The world I knew changed in an instant, and I felt suspended in time and place. It is in those moments of physical and emotional derailment when we, like the exiles of Psalm 137, feel our footing give; we find ourselves on foreign soil even in the places we used to feel safe and secure. And like the Levite singers of our Psalm who hang up their lyres, we often find ourselves unable to do what normally comes so naturally. At best, we are able to "go through the motions" in order to function as expected.

The poet gives us important advice. What do the recent exiles in our Psalm do in this moment? All they can do in that moment: weep. They cry out aloud. These opening verses remind us of one of the critical steps in transitioning to a place of healing after trauma. Mourning.

Too often, the natural emotive impulse to mourn is stayed by the command (imposed equally by our self and others) to be strong and resolute in the face of challenge. Psalm 137 counters that notion. Strength does not negate the need to mourn. The image put forth by the psalmist here in these opening lines acknowledges the importance of being present in the moment and acknowledging sadness in the face of loss. It's okay to just sit and weep when confronting pain just as our Israelite ancestors did on the shores of Babylon. Sometimes there is just nothing else to be done in that moment. Healing is a journey, hopefully to a place where we come to terms with our new reality. But it is just that: a journey. At the start, it is appropriate to acknowledge the loss of being in that place where we once felt entirely whole, a place where we may never be again.

The middle verses of Psalm 137 remind us of the importance of memory in this process:

> Should I forget you, Jerusalem,
> may my right hand whither;
> May my tongue cleave to my palate,
> if I do not remember you,
> if I do not set Jerusalem above my chief joy.

So often when we are in pain, all we want to do is forget. The phrases, "put the past behind you," "move on," "you need closure," or "get over it" highlight a natural human inclination towards wanting to build a giant wall between places and moments of trauma and the future. But healing isn't about disconnecting from the things that pain us. Amputation isn't a cure—it's a last resort leading in many cases to remaining phantom pain. Healing is, under ideal circumstances, about mending from the experience of pain. Healing involves reconciling experienced pain and trauma with our self in a manner that allows us to move forward. It's not about "getting over it" or "putting it behind us," it's about being able to move forward through it and with it.

These middle verses make the most impact if we accept the idea that they were indeed penned by one of the Temple musicians (Ahn, 284). Take it from a Cantor: the ability to create and share music is central to a musician's identity; and, for the Temple musician, the music he created was not solely his own but for the community's sake. His identity was fully tied into the rituals and cultic experiences of Temple life. In some ways, we might imagine, it'd be easier for this musician to forget. But the poet is pointedly reminding us, that despite the pain of the past, he (and by extension, we) must remember. To forget, for this lyre player, is to sever a vital limb and his very ability to make music. To forget, for this singer of sacred song, is to go permanently mute, to be unable to sing ever again. To forget is to amputate part of the self. We can't erase pain. We may really want to in the hardest moments but forgetting, more often than not, causes us to risk losing a vital part of who we are.

The challenge with remembering is that it's virtually impossible to remember the goodness of what we experienced before an episode of trauma without being reminded of the trauma itself and the associating pain that surrounds it. Here the last verses of Psalm 137 can be informative. Strikingly, the poet is continuing the theme of remembering even though he is reflecting on the very worst of his trauma. He isn't asking to forget, but (let's also be very clear) he also isn't putting the responsibility to remember these most painful elements of his beloved Jerusalem on himself. Instead, he is placing that burden on something outside of himself and beyond his control, namely on God:

Remember, Adonai, the Edomites
[who] on the day of Jerusalem, said:
'Uncover her, strip her to her foundation.'

Our poet understands the fullness of the pain he carries. It feels too much for him in these immediate moments. This becomes fully clear in the final verses of the Psalm:

Daughter of Babylon the despoiler—
Happy who pays you back in kind
for what you did to us. Happy who seizes
and smashes your infants against the rock.

Robert Alter describes the book of Psalms as "quintessentially a 'poetry of the heart,' a spontaneous outpouring of feeling expressed with directness and simplicity...." (Alter, 112). These final verses certainly confirm Alter's description. They are nothing short of a written outpouring of violent revenge fantasy. There is, as Alter succinctly says, "no moral justification"(ibid., 475), for this concluding image, but we are so eager to cut out this painfully challenging part of the psalm that we forget to consider whether such a fantasy isn't unwarranted. Notice I say "fantasy;" I think we can all agree such actions would be reprehensible under all circumstances. Anger is, however, not only warranted but understandable. If read as emotional outpouring of the soul, these last verses not only give us a more detailed window into the trauma experienced by the author, they also grant us permission to experience and express hurt and utter rage felt in the face of trauma.

Trauma and Expression of Emotional Pain

The horror of that final image of infanticide the psalm offers must be read in the context of what comes in the two verses before it, "Remember God" the things they did to us, and "happy who pays [Babylon] back in kind." In kind. No more, no less. The poet wants his enemy to feel the same pain his community felt when their women were raped, and their children seized and murdered in such barbaric fashion. Again, the psalm isn't advocating for retribution. Rather, it is offering a literary outlet for the full expression of emotional pain. These final verses of Psalm 137 offer us insight into the full horror that the poet himself witnessed, give voice to the expression of rage, and offer a supplication for some element of justice.

What is remarkable to me isn't that this raw expression of emotion was penned. For all we know, there were other similar poetic expressions of rage that didn't make the canonical cut. Expressing oneself and venting raw emotion through writing and journal keeping is a tool recommended by many therapists for processing anger and pain, so it is certainly easy to imagine our ancestors kept their share of writings. What is remarkable is that Psalm 137, a text that belies classification into any typical psalm category and contains a particularly graphic vision of bloody revenge nowhere else seen among the Psalms was considered worthy of inclusion in the book of Psalms. Not only was the text of Psalm 137 canonized, but its placement in the order of psalms is significant; it is part of the story.

As I mentioned early in this chapter, the book of Psalms does not end with Psalm 137. The fantasy of barbaric revenge is not left as the final word on the healing journey of the Babylonian exiles. Psalm 137 is immediately preceded and followed by psalms of gratitude. The experiences of raw anguish and hostility are stages in the process of healing from trauma; messy uncomfortable stages. The Biblical editor recognizes this and reminds us that these stages, with all of their hostility and anger, do not negate the ability for us to once again be able to experience gratitude. Borrowing from Kübler-Ross' terminology again, acceptance is possible. It isn't necessarily (or even probably) permanent, but it is certainly attainable.

"By the waters of Babylon," I sang as a child, not understanding the context of the text or the source of the music I was taught. As a Cantor, I have since encountered many musical arrangements of various verses of Psalm 137; not surprisingly, none include those final verses 7-9 of Psalm 137. However, the music I learned as a child, the 19th-century melody, with the simple rolling canon, reminds me that grief and pain often roll in and out of our lives. Sometimes, those waves roll in and out at times we least expect it. Healing from trauma is simply not a one-and-done proposition. If only it were only that easy. Perhaps that is why the poet who authored Psalm 137 knew well enough to hand over the most frightening and vengeful of his feelings over to God. He may have recognized they'd come back from time to time; and while the feelings were his to experience in their fullness, they weren't his to act upon.

Healing

The goal of healing isn't necessarily resolution. The modern eagerness for "closure" is terribly misleading. Doors more often than not remain open. We generally don't get justice for the bad or painful things that happen to us. We will have reminders that bring us back to places of sadness and even anger. At the same time, as unfair as it sounds, it is our responsibility to deal with the impact of those bad things that happen to us. A door that we must always keep open is the willingness to seek out and accept assistance in dealing with the full spectrum of emotions that come from the experience of trauma. It is our responsibility to deal with it. It is not a path we must endure alone.

Psalm 137 is a challenging text. It is also a deeply human one that reminds us that healing (as defined by the ability to move forward beyond trauma), comes from that ability to sit with and face even the messiest of our emotions—loss, alienation from one's core identity, sadness, bitterness, and even rage—and still look in the mirror and accept ourselves as wholly and holy human.

Psalm 150
Gratitude

Translation and Interpretation by
Rabbi Dr. Rafael Goldstein, BCC

1. Halleluyah!
      Praise God in God's sanctuary;
      Praise God in the firmament of God's power.
2. Praise God for God's mighty acts;
      Praise God as befits God's might acts.
3. Praise God with blasts of the horn;
      Praise God with harp and lyre.
4. Praise God with timbrel and dance;
      Praise God with lute and flute.
5. Praise God with resounding cymbals;
      Praise God with loud-crashing cymbals.
6. Let all that breathes praise the Holy One.
      Halleluyah!

Psalms in the Key of Healing

הַלְלוּ יָהּ | הַלְלוּ־אֵל בְּקָדְשׁוֹ הַלְלוּהוּ בִּרְקִיעַ עֻזּוֹ:
הַלְלוּהוּ בִגְבוּרֹתָיו הַלְלוּהוּ כְּרֹב גֻּדְלוֹ:
הַלְלוּהוּ בְּתֵקַע שׁוֹפָר הַלְלוּהוּ בְּנֵבֶל וְכִנּוֹר:
הַלְלוּהוּ בְתֹף וּמָחוֹל הַלְלוּהוּ בְּמִנִּים וְעוּגָב:
הַלְלוּהוּ בְצִלְצְלֵי־שָׁמַע הַלְלוּהוּ בְּצִלְצְלֵי תְרוּעָה:
כֹּל הַנְּשָׁמָה תְּהַלֵּל יָהּ הַלְלוּ־יָהּ

Dr. Elizabeth Kubler Ross wrote of five stages of loss or of dying: denial, anger, bargaining, depression, acceptance (Kubler-Ross, 19700. However, her stages reflect only part of the process. Thankfulness and gratitude are critical to completing the process. In working with bereavement groups, I learned that the best way to help determine when a person was done with the group was when they could say they were grateful for what they had, and grateful for the ways they had grown since their loss. The process of what they went through was not what they would have wanted, but the realization that they were still alive and have potential for a quality life without the person they lost marked the end of their need for a bereavement group.

Gratitude for what one had (even if it was for less time than one wanted), or gratitude for the process of recovery from loss or grief (even if it is not the way one would have wanted to experience life), or gratitude for surviving in whatever way one has, demonstrates an end of the grief process. Gratitude can also be informative for the ways in which people living with serious illness experience recovery from illness, or the ways in which families experience the loss of a loved one knowing that everything possible was done on their loved one's behalf, whatever that might mean.

Gratitude makes a difference when people decide how satisfied they are with their experience or their treatment by a doctor, hospital, nurse, chaplain, etc. Gratitude can help sustain people experiencing challenges. There is a Jewish tradition of saying 100 blessings per day, as a way of being aware of and counting one's blessings. Counting our blessings is supposed to be a part of our everyday routine, but we really need to do it when we are faced with challenges.

Rabbi Nachman of Bratslav said that gratitude is the antidote for depression.

Personally, I did not expect to get cancer, especially lung cancer, when I never had so much as a puff of a cigarette. The cause for biliary cancer is really unknown, so I could not have expected it either. I would rather not have had this experience. But I am grateful for what I had in terms of my health while I had it, and I am grateful for what I learned about myself and others since my diagnosis. Most importantly, I learned that my siblings really care about me, that some friendships are beyond measure, and I can somehow find the strength to hope and be realistic at the same time. I am grateful for the Holy One helping me find a way through this.

Psalm 150 is about being grateful for whatever you have and experiencing gratitude with everything you can; letting gratitude permeate your body and soul; making gratitude override all other feelings.

"Halleluyah!
Praise God in God's sanctuary;
Praise God in the firmament of God's power."

We have to look again at Psalm 27 to remember where God's sanctuary/dwelling place is. God dwells within and outside of us; we are God's dwelling place, God's sanctuary. When we say "halleluyah"(praise God), we are acknowledging both the God part of us, and the part of God that is us. Praise God not just with the words or thoughts, but from deeply within, with all of our being. The second half of the phrase, "the firmament of God's power" is the external part of God that is beyond us. So, the two lines we praise God with everything you've got, both inside and outside, acknowledging that we are God's sanctuary, but we also live in God's external Presence.

Praising God is an expression of gratitude. By acknowledging and praising, we are thanking God. In this case, the praise, the gratitude, comes from our innermost being, deep within ourselves.

The praise is transcendent of the moment—we praise and thank, express our gratitude, even when the reasons for feeling gratitude may be elusive. It's hard to thank God when one is in the midst of illness, or other personal problems or disaster. It's hard to praise and thank when one doesn't feel gratitude when one is suffering. This expression of gratitude is not necessarily about the present but can be about both the past and the future. As we saw in Psalm 103, "as far as east is from west" we see here a sense of "as far as past is from future," that all one needs is to turn around, to change perspective (as in Psalm 121) and see the gratitude for what was and the hope (Psalm 121) for what will be.

We don't have to appreciate or feel anything about a current situation, since either it will pass or our attitude/perspective could change. We might find the blessings that might be hidden inside what we perceived as a curse, or we might find hope for something better. In any case, we praise God to express gratitude for the good we experienced in the past, for the challenges we might have experienced, for giving us hope for a better future

There is a story in the Talmud about the Temple in Jerusalem. It had one entrance and one exit. Everyone who was well and whole was invited to enter through the main entrance. But people who were in mourning, ill, disabled, or sad for whatever reason were supposed to enter through the exit. At first this seems pretty unfair. But think about the process.

When the people who are well go through the process of being in the Temple, they are transformed by the experience. They leave, and who do they see? The very people in need of that transformation the most. They greet the infirm and the sad and say to them, "Go in, this is a great place where you will find strength and hope. May you be comforted and transformed like me in the process!" The infirm and sad go in through the exit so they can be comforted on the way in.

When they leave the Temple, going out the entrance, who do they see? The people who are well. They say to them "Go on in! This is a great and meaningful place. May you be comforted and transformed like me in the process!"

"Praise God for God's mighty acts; Praise God as befits God's mighty acts."

God's mighty acts could be the things God did for our people in the Bible, like creation stories, or the Ten Plagues, or splitting the Red Sea so we could escape the pursuing Egyptians. These are the traditional understandings of God's mighty acts; yet, as we personalize these psalms and understand them not just from a historical point of view, God's mighty acts might be the renewal of creation within each and every one of us.

As was mentioned earlier in this chapter, we are supposed to say 100 blessings a day. Can it be that each of these blessings could count among God's mighty acts? We woke up this morning despite the possible odds against such an event. We remembered who we are, ate, dressed, went to the bathroom, did the things we usually see as routine, until suddenly our ability to do any of these things might be challenged. Then we know first-hand that what once seemed routine and "normal" could actually reflect a mighty act of God. I'm not suggesting a theology of God being involved in the minutiae of our daily lives, but am recognizing that some driving force is enabling me to move forward with my life. That force I will never understand, but I would consider it to be one of the mighty acts of God.

As I think of God's mighty acts I also note that lots of other people reflect them, which may have brought them into healing professions, professions of research, support for the healers, or into arts and entertainment, so we have reflections of the beauty and challenges of life. When we say a blessing, like *hamotzi lehem min ha'aretz*, thanking God for bringing forth bread from the earth, we know bread doesn't grow on vines. It is our partnership with God that turns the crops into edible food, but think of the hundreds of people who are involved in the process: the farmer, the farmer's equipment makers, the banks who provide the funding for the farmers to buy their equipment; the plow manufacturers and the truckers who bring the plow to the farm; the farm hands and the people who keep them alive and fed.

Once the crops leave the farm, they go to mills, via truckers who use roads that had to be built, and there were road workers involved in that; plus the people who designed the roads, the people who mixed the tar and rocks or cement and rocks, or who quarried the rocks, and the people who made all of their equipment; the people who educated and took care of all of the above, by building houses, sewer and water systems, utility systems, and removed their garbage. Then there are the bakers who combine the ingredients which come from multiple other sources which rely on yet more people to make their work happen: chicken farmers for the eggs, manufacturers of yeast, nuts or other grains that go into the bread, and again, all of the people who make their work possible.

We still haven't begun to consider the people who turn it into final products and bring those products to market. Or the consumers and all that goes into enabling us to pay $3.29 for a loaf of bread.

When you consider all the people working to bring a simple loaf of bread into our houses, it really is amazing, and that amazement leads me to credit the Holy One for mighty acts, which enable us to work together towards the same goals, taking care of ourselves and others at the same time. We do God's work with our own hands.

"Praise God with blasts of the shofar (horn); Praise God with harp and lyre."

Most Jewish people are familiar with the sounds of the *shofar*, and it makes sense that the rousing sound would be the first musical instrument listed in this psalm. The sound of the shofar can be alarming; can arouse emotions. The shofar is blown on Rosh Hashanah and the month before to prepare us for the personal reflection of the Days of Awe. The shofar is also a natural instrument, a hollowed out ram's horn. The sound is visceral. It cannot be ignored.

There are three traditional sounds that are used for the Days of Awe. The first sound is alarming, almost like a scream. The second blast sounds like when one begins to cry. It is broken into 6 parts. The third blast is completely broken — at least 9 staccato tones. Think of it as the rapid breathing of deep sobbing. All the sounds inspire awe, but what does it mean to praise God when one is in fear, or crying, or feeling broken? When we are broken, even when we are crying, we can find a way to praise God, to turn to God to help us see the other side of the coin, the balance to our sadness. Praise God from the depths of sadness, alarm, and brokenness, which are all part of the human experience, but not the definition of that experience.

Praising God with harp and lyre is easier to understand (though neither instrument looks in the Bible like what it looks like today). Each instrument has comforting and rousing tones. The lyre was the instrument David used to comfort King Saul when he had bouts of depression and anxiety. It is an instrument with 4, 7 or up to 10 strings, maybe in a horseshoe or a box shape. The strings are made from the guts of sheep. Praising God with a lyre implies praising God from your own guts, from deep inside yourself.

The strings on the lyre are plucked by the fingers and can also be strummed. The fingers can have multiple meanings, but I like to think of fingers as the way we get our hands to work: the details. Plucking on the guts with the details of our hands implies an intensity of the praise for God, from our depths and with concern for detail.

The harp looks nothing like the harp we are used to seeing (like Harpo Marx's instrument). That kind of harp was invented in the Renaissance. The harp of Biblical times was bow shaped and could not withstand the tension of the 47 strings we are used to seeing. Harps had more strings than lyres and produced louder sounds and had more musical options in making music. We often associate harps with calming music. In addition to strings made of guts, harps used metallic strings as well, made of copper or brass. Harps are plucked or strummed enabling the musician greater musical expression than with a lyre. Again, they make their sounds using fingers. The action of praising God with harp is to bring a fullness of sound, using the fingers to make the music.

"Praise God with timbrel and dance; Praise God with lute and flute."

A timbrel is a two-sided, hand-held drum, like a tambourine but without the small pieces of metal on the sides that make them jangle. Depending on how one hits the skin on either side, there are different tones a timbrel might have. As a drum in the Ancient Near East, the timbrel was made by stretching dried skins over a wood frame. The symbolism for praising God with a timbrel is praising God with everything inside your own skin. The shape of the timbrel—round—may also symbolize one's head or one's belly.

Despite having a list of musical instruments to praise God, there is also praising God with dance. How is dance a musical instrument? Certainly, we can think of the sounds that can be made using tap shoes, stomping, or dragging feet. And the idea of movement to music—dance—enables one to envision praising God with one's whole body. This musical instrument of dance involves the entire body in the process making the sounds to praise God. (As I type this, I notice the rhythm of the sounds my keyboard makes, the sounds of the interactions of body parts on inanimate objects, like feet in floors. I am also thinking about the scene in *Singing in the Rain* when Gene Kelly puts newspapers on the floor and tears them with his feet while dancing to the rhythm.)

Both the lute and flute make very distinct sounds and in very different ways: one has to be plucked, the other is a wind instrument. Both employ the use of the hands/fingers. The flute is not like the flute we see today. It was more akin to what we now call a "recorder," a much simpler instrument. To blow it, one would hold it in front of one's body (not to the side as with a modern flute) and use fingers to cover holes to modulate the tone. This flute differs with the shofar/horn in that the only way to modulate the tones of the shofar is through the embouchure (the positioning of the mouth, jaw, tongue, and lips). The flute uses fingers and breath, working together.

The lute looks like a guitar with a big belly and bent neck. It has 6 to 12 strings which can be modulated by the pressing the strings against the neck to shorten them, thus raising their tones. Although modern lutes have frets, the frets were probably a much later addition to the instrument. The major difference between the lyre, harp, and lute would be that the sound of each string of the lute can be modulated by the fingers, which cannot happen with either the lyre or the harp. The commonality between the flute and the lute is that the tones of each can be modulated by the fingers.

"Praise God with resounding cymbals;
Praise God with loud-crashing cymbals."

Resounding symbols would be similar to the cymbals we have today—metallic objects that make a wonderful crashing sound when they crash. They resound because they vibrate and one can feel the vibration endure and fade with the sound of the crash. Pulsating sounds can resonate as a heartbeat. Cymbals can startle.

Loud-crashing cymbals are very different—they are what we would call gongs. They produce a deep, resonant, multi-tonal sustained sound, and the vibrations can be felt from quite a distance from the instrument. Gongs can awaken and inspire awe. Percussion instruments are about vibrations, actually enabling us to feel the sound inside ourselves. They can lead one to wonder about spiritual vibrations. One can feel the resounding vibes throughout one's body.

The instruments all represent different body parts—and involve different body parts in making their sounds. The clear message of all of the instruments is to involve oneself fully and totally, from inside out, in praising God. The instruments encourage us to feel God's "vibe" within ourselves and to resonate with it using our breath, fingers, mouths and faces, our feet and legs, our innards. The timbrel uses skin, reminding us of everything inside our skin is praising God. The lute reminds us of our bellies (so does the shape of the timbrel). The flute voice reminds us of our voices. Our feet and dance again remind us that our entire bodies are involved. All the strings could be that which binds us all together, or even strings that place us in bondage. The cymbals represent the sparkle of our personalities, the ability each of us has to make an impression, to resonate, to make others "vibe" with us. The body is not just praising God but is *being* the praise for God and of God. *We* are the praise!

There is another action at play here. While the previous discussion focused on each instrument individually, this psalm is encouraging us to be an orchestra together—to praise God with everything we each have as individuals but to also praise God with everything we have as a community—to raise our collective voices and collective instruments together in a magnificent "Ode to Joy." To be heard as an individual, but also as part of something much bigger: a sound we cannot make alone. We need the other voices and instruments to make the best and most meaningful sounds.

We are the praise for God and of God in our massive chorus/orchestra!

"Let all that breathes praise the Holy One. Halleluyah!"

The translation for this last line can have two completely different meanings:

1. Let all that breathes praise the Holy One.
   (The breathers are praising.)
2. Let every breath praise the Holy One.
   (Each breath praises.)

Neither is exclusive of the other. "Let all that breathes" praise God includes all living things praising God, while "let every breath" praise God changes the direct object from the beings that breathe to the breath itself being a form of praise. Either way, praising God is associated with life, with breathing, and connecting with the Holy One through breath. After all, inanimate objects and the dead have no ability to praise God, but our very breathing, our living, is a form of praise for God. Just breathing, living another cycle of inhaling and exhaling, is a form of praising God. And neither is exclusively about human beings—all living things breathe. We share breathing with our pets, our food animals, our non-food animals, fish and all that lives underwater, our pests, even our trees. All living things are a form of praise for God.

The formulation here does not leave a lot of room for argument—everything that lives, by definition, is a form of praise for God, the Creator; every breath, no matter how labored or challenged, is a form of praising God. When we are sick, and our lives are threatened, even when we experience breathing problems, each breath, every breath, is a form of connecting with and therefore praising God. Continuing to breathe is an expression of gratitude for the ability to do so.

Everything that is alive praises God. Living in and of itself is a form of praise of God. Despite whatever challenges we might be facing, despite whatever disappointments we may have in our lives, despite any suffering we may be experiencing, life itself is praising God, whether we are conscious or even in agreement with the praise. As long as we are breathing, it counts as praise of God.

Praising God is an expression of gratitude. Halleluyah literally means "praise God," and is contained in every line of this psalm. Praising God is thanking God. Thanking God is also an expression of joy, an expression that there is good to celebrate. When expressing praise and gratitude we can and should feel joy in the process, in knowing and experiencing the gratitude. If we are truly grateful, there is cause for celebration. When people are experiencing sadness, illness, loss, they may not feel the joy at that moment, but can remember and be reminded of joys of the past or hope for joy in the future.

The multitude of instruments listed in the psalm express joy. Individually. and as an orchestra, the experience of all of these instruments and voices together is a joyous experience. Participation in public expressions of thanks — joining others — can also lift our spirits to enable us to express our joy, even when it's part of the group experience rather than the personal experience. We are lifted by the spirit of others when we need it and contribute to the lifting of others' spirits when we can.

Did you ever wonder why geese fly in a V formation? They utilize the airstreams created by the birds in front of them to make flying easier and enable them to go further with less effort. When the lead goose gets tired, another takes over and the lead falls back. In this way, the geese support one another in flight. The same is true for us in prayer: we are boosted by the spirits of others, sometimes able to take the lead, sometimes in need of others to let us glide in their airstream. When we are praising God, and expressing our gratitude, we may be in the lead, in the middle, or at the very end.

There is a common expression, "It's all good." This psalm seems to resonate with this phrase. Everything is for the good, even when we don't personally see the good at any given moment. We can trust that in our flock or in our orchestra the experience of good is there, and there is possibility for participating in the gratitude for the good, if not our own, the good others may be experiencing.

We learn from our difficulties and challenges. There is something about disease, illness or suffering that teaches; there are things we might otherwise not have known about or understood. There can be good hidden within that which appears only to be bad. Gratitude sometimes is the route through which we realize that which we never expected. As I described Rebecca (a Pentecostal Bishop) in the introduction to this book, her illness and suffering brought her closer to Jesus' suffering. She was able to finally understand his suffering better and welcomed it, even as no one would ever wish for it. I noted that there is an incident described in the Talmud in which a rabbi asks his colleague "Is your suffering meaningful to you." I told her I never understood that question until that moment. While not welcome, her suffering was indeed meaningful. It was helping her understand her faith better and to put her faith into action, even if it was incredibly painful.

Pulling It All Together

We can be grateful even when we are suffering. We can experience joy, even if it is vicariously, even if it is in memory or in hope. We can be grateful for what we learned, what we are learning, and what we will learn through challenges, illness and sadness. When we express our gratitude.

This psalm encourages us to put all we have personally into the process of expressing our gratitude. It encourages us to join with others in expressing their gratitude because the process will lift our spirits when we need it, and we can lift the spirits of others when they need it, and we have something to offer them. Gratitude doesn't have to be for the present moment but can be in the memory of that which we are grateful for—in our past or our hopes for our future.

Afterword

Rabbi J.B. Sacks

Rafael was one of my closest family-members-of-choice for well over thirty years. We met back on the East Coast when I was serving Congregation B'nai Jacob in Jersey City, and he had moved from Cincinnati to work as a fundraiser at MetroWest, a large Jewish Federation. He said something to me that was at once provocative, personal, and hit close to home. He had a way of doing that, perhaps to test my reaction, but perhaps also to see how real I was and wasn't. I tried to hide my shock, and I remember actually asking him about his question, what he thought I might need to be pondering more, and what he thought he could learn by the provocation. He was surprised; apparently few people had been that calm in replying. Then we started laughing, deeply, robustly—a laughing that continued for sometime. After that we spoke for a long time, and that began a lifelong *friendship-that-was-family* in which I grew from most every encounter.

He always had a great sense of humor. When he arrived at my home early to meet for lunch, I had just arrived from the gym. I jumped into the shower, quickly dressed, and returned some fifteen minutes later to discover that my living room furniture was entirely rearranged. He decided to teach my Guatemalan-born son Evan Spanish, and a young Evan came home calling out to me what he thought was "Dad." It was actually *Abuelita*— "dear little grandmother."

Psalms in the Key of Healing

Rafael and I were there mostly *with* and always *for* each other during all the peaks and valleys of our lives. I think we thought we had been through about everything—including the demise of my first husband, Melvin Lloyd Rosen, of blessed memory, to AIDS/HIV, along with literally hundreds of our closest friends, companions, coworkers, neighbors, community members.

Considering the enormity of AIDS/HIV epidemic, Rafael found that his fundraising work seemed less important, less vital, than previously. I immediately started to get him involved with New Jersey Buddies, God's Care We Deliver and other organizations to channel his passion to help others. While he could be silly, he had obvious natural skills and a heart that was always open and wide enough to bring in everyone. I have no idea how many people he personally visited—at hospitals and at home—how many people he fed, how many people he shopped for, how many people he delivered meals to, how many people he bathed, how many people he was able to help explore their emotional structure and their spiritual capacity. I know that he always had time for Mel or for me, coming at a moment's notice even well into the night, although he lived a good 30-minute drive from our home.

All his work was imbued with holiness. And when he became a rabbi, he became humbler. But when he got involved in chaplaincy work, he truly found his niche. He became gentler.

So, it was devastating when he got a diagnosis of cancer, and it was frustrating as he never seemed to get a clear sense of exactly which kind of cancer he had. But he tried to gamely take in whatever came next. He truly lived up to the words of the Psalmist (118:17), *Lo amut ki ech-ye, va-asaper ma'asei Yah,* "I shall not die, but I will live, and I shall tell of God's deeds." Think about it: "I shall not die, but I shall live" is the defiant motto of the soul who resists their demise with every ounce of their energy and resolve. Rafael challenged his diagnosis and resisted his decline with all the tenacity and grace that he had within him.

And what does one do with the life that they have gained by taking up the "I shall not die" mantra? Well, if you're Rafael, you do what the psalmist urges: "Proclaim God's deeds." He went and did that by taking up his calling even more. He continued to teach, lead, pray, sing, tell jokes, and rage at injustice. And he decided to write this book, so filled with his personality and humor, yes, but also filled with his humanity, his wisdom, his insight, his Torah. What a gift.

Rabbi Milton Steinberg, *z"l*, taught that we can transcend death in many ways: 1 biologically, through children; in thought, through the survival of our memory; in influence, by virtue of the continuance of our personality as a force among those who come after us; and ideally, through our identification with the timeless things of the spirit. Yet its primary meaning, Steinberg reminds us, is that what survives is our consciousness, our essential personality, our soul.[1]

Rafael has died but has not died, for he has transcended death in all the ways that Rabbi Steinberg elaborates:

While Rafael did not have children, he raised up a generation of students, who are now chaplains and serving people not only of their faith traditions, but people of any and no faith. Through his teaching and mentoring of chaplains, he lived up to the Talmudic dictum, "The one who mentors another is considered as having sired them."[2]

Rafael was a larger-than-life figure. He was one of those people who once you've met him, you do not forget him. He will survive, then, in thought. He also survives in influence, for the kind of wisdom and Torah he bore, as exhibited in this book. His approach to Psalms and the way he could discover new levels of meaning and depth in a verse, a phrase, a word— opened up new layers not only within the text but within our souls.

191

Rafael, too, identified more and more with "the timeless things of the spirit," as the reader has surely discovered: life, love, self-acceptance, forgiveness, reconciliation, working through grief, hope, joy, and more.

In his life, in his work, and in his writings he was a model for all of us. The work he helped us to do was the work he continued to do on himself. And, in the last phase of his life, he managed to do what the Jewish tradition challenges: to *chok'varo*, to align our entire beings, our outside with our inside, our presentation to the world with our hearts' reality.[3] He aligned his heart, mind, and soul with each other, with the universe, and with God. And in so doing, there is hope that we, too, might so evolve and live

Rafael's consciousness, his spiritual capacity, his soul, has left this life as it was brought in: pure, and pure light. And we who have basked in it, even if only by reading this book, can start to sense our lives "in the key of healing."

Kein y'hi ratzon. So may it be for all of us.

Notes

1 *Basic Judaism* (Harcourt, Brace and World, 1960), p. 160.

2 BT Sanhedrin 19b. The statement is credited to Rabbi Yonatan.

3 BT Yoma 72b. Cf. Maimonides, *Mishneh Torah,* Laws of Personal Character 2:6.

Bibliography

Ahn, John. "Psalm 137: Complex Communal Laments." Journal of Biblical Literature 127, no. 2 (2008): 267-289.

Alter, Robert. *The Book of Psalms: A Translation with Commentary.* New York, NY: Norton 2007.

Aronson, Louise. *Elderhood.* New York, N.Y.: Bloomsbury Publishing, 2019.

Brueggeman, Walter. *Spirituality of the Psalms.* Minneapolis, MN: Fortress Press, 2002.

Campbell, Don. *Music Physician for Times to Come.* Wheaton, IL: Quest Books, 1991.

Campbell, Don. *The Mozart Effect: Tapping the Power of Music to Heal the Body, Strengthen the Mind, and Unlock the Creative Spirit.* New York: HarperCollins, 2001.

Chiel, Samuel and Dreher, Henry. *For Thou Art With Me: The Healing Power of Psalms: Renewal, Recovery and Acceptance from the World's Most Beloved Ancient Verses.* New York: Rodale, 2000.

Dahood, Mitchell. *The Anchor Bible Series Psalms III: 101-150.* Garden City, NY: Doubleday, 1966.

Dittes, James E. *Pastoral Couseling: The Basics.* Louisville KY, Westminster John Knox Press, 1999.

Doehring, Carrie. *The Practice of Pastoral Care: A Postmodern Approach.* Louisville, KY:Westminster/John Knox Press, 2006.

Dorff, Elliot. *Knowing God: Jewish Journeys to the Unknowable.* New Jersey: Aronson, 1992.

Duncan, King, ed. *Dynmaic Preaching* 13, no 3 (Oct-Dec., 1997).

Dykstra, Robert C. *Images of Pastoral Care: Classic Readings.* St. Louis, MO: Chalice Press, 1990.

Psalms in the Key of Healing

Ephraim, Rabbi Moshe Chaim of Sudlikov, *Degel Machaneh Ephraim*. n.d (1810).

Frankel, Estelle. *Sacred Therapy: Jewish Spiritual Teachings on Emotional Healing and Inner Wholeness*. Boston: Shambhala Press, 2003.

Frankl, Viktor. *Man's Search for Meaning: An Introduction to Logotherapy*. New York: Touchstone Books, 1984.

Freedman, David Noel. *"The Structure of Psalm 137."* In *Near Eastern Studies in Honor of William Foxwell Albright*, edited by Hans Goedicke, 187-205. Baltimore: Johns Hopkins Press, 1971. Reprinted in Freedman, D.N. *Pottery, Poetry, & Prophecy Collected Essays on Hebrew Poetry*. Winona Lake, IN: Eisenbrauns, 1980.

Garcia, Joshua R. R. "Healing in Disorientation: A Close Reading of Psalm 137 (Beyond the Babies)." BTI Student Conference: Engaging Rhetorics of Healing April, 2016.

Gaynor, Mitchell L. *The Healing Power of Sound: Recovery from Life-threatening Illness Using Sound, Voice and Music*. Boston, MA: Shambhala Publications Inc., 2002.

Gillman, Neil. *The Way Into Encountering God in Judaism*. Woodstock,VT.: Jewish Lights Publishing, 2000.

Goldstein, Niles. *Lost Souls: Finding Hope in the Heart of Darkness*. New York: Bell Tower, 2002.

Groopman, Jerome. *The Anatomy of Hope: How to Prevail in the Face of Illness*. New York: Random House, 2004.

Hays, Christopher B. "How Shall We Sing? Psalm 137 in Historical and Canonical Context." *Horizons in Biblical Theology* 27. (2005): 35-55.

Hayes, Phillip. *The Muses Delight: Catches, Glees, Canzonets, and Canons*. London: Forgotten Books, 2017 (1786).

Heschel, Abraham Joshua. *God in Search of Man: A Philosophy of Judaism*. New York: Farrar, Straus and Giroux, 1955.

_____. *Between God and Man: An Interpretation of Judaism.* New York: The Free Press, 1959.

_____. *The Insecurity of Freedom: Essays on Human Existence*. New York: Schocken, 1972.

194

Kauffman, Jeffrey. "On The Primacy of Shame." *In The Shame of Death, Grief, and Trauma,* edited by Jeffrey Kauffman, 3-23. New York: Routledge, 2010.

Kübler-Ross, Elisabeth. *On Death and Dying.* New York, NY: Collier Books/Macmillan, 1970.

Kübler Ross, Elisabeth and Kessler, David. *On Grief and Grieving.* New York, NY: Scribner, 2005.

Kushner, Harold. *How Good Do We Have to Be? A New Approach to Guilt and Forgiveness.* New York: Knopf, 1999.

_____. *The Lord is My Shepherd: Healing Wisdom of the Twenty Third Psalm,* New York: Knopf, 2003.

_____. *Conquering Fear: Living Boldly in an Uncertain World.* New York: Knopf, 2009.

_____. *Overcoming Life's Disappointments.* New York, Knopf, 2006

_____. *Conquering Fear: Living Boldly in an Uncertain World.* New York: Knopf, 2009.

Lamm, Rabbi Maurice. *The Power of Hope: The One Essential of Life and Love.* New York, Rawson Associates, 1995.

Lester, Andrew. *Hope in Pastoral Care and Counseling.* London: Westminster/John Knox Press, 1995.

Lindemann, Eric. *Beyond Grief: Studies in Crisis Intervention.* New York: Jason Aaronson, 1979.

Matt, Daniel. *The Essential Kabbalah: The Heart of Jewish Mysticism.* New Jersey: Castle Books, 1990.

Mitchell, Stephen A and Black, Margaret J. *Freud and Beyond: A History of Modern Psychoanalytic Thought.* New York: Basic Books, 1-324, 2016. Kindle.

Mother Teresa. *Come Be My Light: The Private Writings of the Saint of Calcutta.* New York: Image Books, 2009.

Muffs, Yochanan. *The Personhood of God: Biblical Theology, Human Faith and the Divine Image.* Vermont: Jewish Lights, 2005.

Nouwen, Henri. *The Wounded Healer: Ministry in Contemporary Society.* Garden City, NY: Image Books, 1972.

Nuland, Sherwin. *How We Die: Reflections on Life's Final Chapter.* New York: Vintage Books, 1993.

Plaut, Gunther. *The Torah: A Modern Commentary.* New York, NY: UAHC, 1980.

Polish, Daniel. *Bringing the Psalms to Life: How to Understand and Use the Book of Psalms.* Vermont: Jewish Lights, 2000.

Puchalski, Christina, and Betty Ferrell. *Making Healthcare Whole: Integrating Spirituality into Patient Care.* Philadelphia: Templeton Press, 2010.

Rozenberg, Martin S. and Bernard M. Zlotowitz *The Book of Psalms.* Northvale, NJ: Aaronson, 1999.

Schafer, Roy. *Bad Feelings: Selected Psychoanalytic Essays.* New York: Routledge, 2019.

Schulweis, Harold. *For Those Who Can't Believe: Overcoming the Obstacles to Faith.* New York: Harper, 1994.

Schwartz, Dannel I. *Finding Joy: A Practical Spiritual Guide to Happiness.* Vermont: Jewish Lights, 1998.

Schermer, Victor L. "Between Shame, Death, & Mourning: The Predispositional Role of Early Attachments and the Sense of Self." In *The Shame of Death, Grief, and Trauma*, edited by Jeffrey Kauffman, 22-58. New York: Routledge, 2010.

Schwartz, Richard. *Introduction to the Internal Family Systems Model.* Oak Park, IL: Trailheads Publications, 2001.

Sogyal Rinpoche. *The Tibetan Book of Living and Dying.* San Francisco: Harper San Francisco, 1994.

Wolpe, David. *Making Loss Matter: Creating Meaning in Difficult Times.* New York: Penguin Random House, 1999.

About the Editors

Rabbi Dr. H. Rafael Goldstein, BCC received his Doctorate in Ministry (Spiritual Counseling) from Hebrew Union College in 2014. He was ordained by the Academy for Jewish Religion in 1994. He was Board certified by the National Association of Jewish Chaplains (NAJC) in 2004 and by  the Association of Professional Chaplains in 2011.

He served as the Executive Director of Neshamah: Association of Jewish Chaplains (NAJC) from 2016-2019. Prior to NAJC, he was the Director of Clinical Services for the Center for Spirituality and Health of Mount Sinai Health in New York City. He started the with the equivalent of one full-time priest and himself, and was tasked with creating a world-class department of spiritual care. When he left, there were 35 people in the department including students, residents, educators, chaplains, community outreach and the departments of three other Mount Sinai acquired hospitals.

He has served as the Vice President for Jewish Affairs of Jewish Family and Children's Service in Phoenix and the Jewish community Chaplain in San Diego.

Dr. Goldstein is the author of four books, including *Being a Blessing: 54 Ways You Can Help People Living with Illness.* He is lead or co-author of four peer-reviewed articles in medical journals.

Rabbi Dr. J.B. Sacks currently serves as the spiritual leader of Congregation Am HaYam in Ventura, California, and also serves as Education and Curriculum Specialist for the Stories of Music Project of the UCLA Herb Alpert School of Music, in conjunction with the Lowell Milken Archives of Jewish Music. He served for 10 years at de Toledo High School (West Hills, CA), where he taught in the

Psalms in the Key of Healing

Jewish Studies Department, chairing the Tanakh track and serving as the Director of Jewish Life. Rabbi Sacks also served as the Director of Outreach Publications, as Librarian, and as chair of the Faculty Committee on Pluralism and Inclusion.

Rabbi Sacks has received graduate degrees from the University of Judaism (now American Jewish University) and the Jewish Theological Seminary of America (JTS) in New York City, where he received his ordination. He received his Doctor of Ministry degree from Claremont School of Theology, where he completing his dissertation with a spiritual commentary on Psalm 32. JTS conferred an honorary Doctor of Divinity degree upon Rabbi Sacks.

A long-time advocate of tolerance and inclusion with Jewish life, Rabbi Sacks has co-edited two volumes: *We See Ourselves as Redeemed: A Liberation Haggadah* (1996) and *Ka-Afikim Ba-Negev: A Manual for Rabbis in Engaging Their Communities in Embracing Gay and Lesbian Jews* (1994). He has published articles on various Jewish topics., and has developed a number of creative rituals.

Rabbi Sacks served for many years on the Faculty of the Academy for Jewish Religion, California (AJRCA), heading the Department of Jewish Philosophy and teaching future Jewish chaplains, cantors, and rabbis. Rabbi Sacks lives with his husband Steven Karash in Palm Desert, California. They have an adult son, Evan.

About the Contributors

Rabbi Richard F. Address is the Founder and Director of *www. jewishsacredaging.com*. Rabbi Address served for over three decades on the staff of the Union for Reform Judaism; first as a Regional Director and then, beginning in 1997, as Founder and Director of the URJ's Department of Jewish Family Concerns and served as a specialist and consultant for the North American Reform Movement in the areas of family-related programming. Rabbi Address was ordained from Hebrew Union College-Jewish Institute of Religion in 1972 and began his rabbinic career in Los Angeles congregations. He also served as a part-time rabbi for Beth Hillel in Carmel, NJ while regional director and, after his URJ tenure, served as senior rabbi of Congregation M'kor Shalom in Cherry Hill, NJ from 2011-2014.

Rabbi Address's work has focused on the development and implementation of the project on Sacred Aging. This project has been responsible for creating awareness and resources for congregations on the implication of the emerging longevity revolution with growing emphasis on the aging of the baby boomer generation. This aging revolution has begun to impact all aspects of Jewish communal and congregational life.

Rabbi Address was ordained at the Hebrew Union College-Jewish Institute of Religion (HUC-JIR) in Cincinnati in 1972 and served congregations in California before joining the staff of the Union for Reform Judaism (formerly the Union of American Hebrew Congregations) in 1978. He directed the Union's Pennsylvania Council from 1978 through 2000. In 1997 he founded the Department of Jewish Family Concerns and went full time in New York in January of 2001.

Psalms in the Key of Healing

Rabbi Address received a Certificate in Pastoral Counseling from the Post Graduate Center for Mental Health in 1998. He recieved a Doctor of Ministry HUC-JIR in 1999 and an honorary Doctorate of Divinity (1997) from HUC-JIR.

In January of 2007 Rabbi Address was awarded the "Sherut L'Am" award by the Kalsman Institute for Judaism and Health. He teaches classes in Jewish Family issues and Sacred Aging at the New York campus of HUC-JIR. In March 2010, Rabbi Address was awarded a Best Practices in Older Adult Programs: First Place by the National Council on Aging-Interfaith Coalition on Aging.

Rabbi Address contributes articles for web sites on issues related to spirituality and aging. He co-chairs the Committee on Spirituality and Diversity for C-TAC (Coalition to Transform Advanced Care), and serves as Rabbinic Advisor to Men of Reform Judaism. For four years, he hosted a weekly radio show in Philadelphia called "Boomer Generation Radio," which is archived in podcast form. Beginning in winter 2018, Rabbi Address began hosting a weekly podcast, *Seekers of Meaning*, dedicated to discussing issues related to aging, spirituality, and the impact on families, and congregations. Rabbi Address has authored numerous articles, book chapters and books related to the issue of aging.

Rabbi Dayle Friedman, BCC is a pioneer in the development of a Jewish spiritual vision for aging, spiritual care and healing. She was the founding director of *Hiddur: The Center for Aging and Judaism* at the Reconstructionist Rabbinical College, which provided education, spiritual resources, and scholarship for elders and their caregivers She offers spiritual direction, classes, training, and consulting through Growing Older, her Philadelphia-based national practice. She was ordained by the Hebrew Union College-Jewish Institute of Religion in 1985. From 1985 until 1997 she was the founding director of chaplaincy services at the Philadelphia Geriatric Center.

Rabbi Friedman's books include *Jewish Wisdom for Growing Older: Finding Your Grit and Grace Beyond Midlife, Jewish Visions for Aging: A Professional Guide for Fostering Wholeness*, with Eugene B. Borowitz and Thomas R. Cole and *Jewish Pastoral Care: A Practical Handbook from Traditional and Contemporary Sources*

Rabbi Friedman was listed among The Forward's 50 most influential American Jews in 2008 and its 50 most influential American women rabbis in 2010. Rabbi Friedman has recieved two honorary Doctor of Divinity degrees, from the Hebrew Union College-Jewish Institute of Religion and from the Reconstructionist Rabbinical College.

In 2011 she received the Religion, Spirituality and Aging Award from the American Society on Aging.

Cantor Rabbi Dr. Rhoda J. Harrison was ordained as a cantor and rabbi and recieved her Masters of Sacred Music degree in 1993 by the Hebrew Union College-Jewish Institute of Religion. She currently serves Congregation M'kor Shalom in Cherry Hill, New Jersey. Prior to moving to New Jersey, Harrison served the Reform community in Baltimore, MD for 25 years at the former Har Sinai and Temple Emanuel congregations. Harrison earned her Doctorate in Jewish Studies in 2012 from Towson University. Her areas of specialization were Liturgy and classical Hebrew, and she wrote her dissertation on the *Accommodation of the Seder Avodah of Yom Kippur to Modernity*.

Rabbi Dr. Shira Stern, BCC is a pastoral counselor and Disaster Spiritual Care provider for the American Red Cross. As the Director of the Center for Pastoral Care and Counseling in Marlboro, New Jersey, she works with children and adults as they focus on problem solving and personal growth. Rabbi Stern has more than 32 years of educational experience, including teaching Judaism at Rutgers University. She earned a Bachelor of Arts degree from Brown University and a Master of Arts degree from Hebrew Union College, where she was ordained a rabbi. She earned her Doctor of Ministry degree in Pastoral Counseling from HUC-JIR in 2003. She is also a Board Certified Chaplain, and has served as a hospital, hospice, and long-term care facility chaplain. Rabbi Stern's writings have been published in *The Women's Torah Commentary* and *The Women's*

Psalms in the Key of Healing

Haftarah Commentary, Jewish Relational Care from A-Z, and she is the consulting editor of *Mishkan R'fuah, Where Healing Resides,* published by the Central Conference of American Rabbis. She has been a contributor and consultant for three National Geographic Books.

202

Made in the USA
Middletown, DE
26 April 2021

37963897R00130